PATRC

D0462156

HANDBOOK

THE

PATRON SAINTS
HANDBOOK

BY

MITCH FINLEY

theWORD
among us®
press

Published by The Word Among Us Press
9639 Doctor Perry Road
Ijamsville, Maryland 21754
www.wau.org

ISBN: 978-1-59325-169-7
14 13 12 11 10   1 2 3 4 5

Unless otherwise noted, Scripture passages contained herein are from the New Revised Standard Version Bible: Catholic Edition, copyright © 1989, 1993, Division of Christian Education of the National Council of the Churches of Christ in the United States. All rights reserved. Used with permission.

Cover design by John Hamilton

Library of Congress Cataloging-in-Publication Data

Finley, Mitch.
  The patron saints handbook / Mitch Finley.
    p. cm.
  Includes bibliographical references (p.   ) and index.
  ISBN 978-1-59325-169-7 (alk. paper)
  1. Christian patron saints. I. Title.
  BX4656.5.F56 2010
  270.092'2--dc22
                          2010028321

CONTENTS

INTRODUCTION

Saints don't go out of style, and patron saints in particular enjoy a perennial popularity, a few even among members of Protestant denominations and even other religions. Something about the saints attracts and intrigues us. Perhaps it's their special closeness to the mystery of the divine, or their simplicity, or their inclination to thumb their noses at the pretensions of power and wealth. Sometimes they endear themselves to people by their common sense and good humor. Even the saints who were dour or utterly impractical fascinate us.

The Catholic affection for saints was what led to the tradition of adopting saints as patrons of particular causes, groups, or regions. In *The Patron Saints Handbook*, you'll learn about one hundred such saints. You'll find out, for example, who St. Genesius was and why he is the patron saint of actors. You'll discover why St. Thérèse of Lisieux, who spent her life in a cloistered French convent, is the patron saint of missionaries. You'll meet the patron saint of firefighters, songwriters—and even astronauts.

Before we go any further on the topic of patron saints, however, we need to have a clear understanding of saints in general and their role in the life of the community of faith. The saints are recommended to us because they excelled at living their lives with great trust and confidence in God. As they willingly and completely opened their hearts to the risen Christ, God was able to do marvelous, frequently delightful, and always inspiring things through them. Because of their heroic virtue, the Church recognizes them as worthy of devotion. That's why they're saints.

At the same time, saints are like anyone who has ever lived in this world and died trusting in the grace of Christ: They live now as they lived then, as members of the Church, the same faith community to which we belong. This is what Catholic tradition calls "the communion of saints," and we who flounder around in time and space are every bit as much members of this communion as are the countless souls who went before us. Just as we may ask others here in time and space to pray for us, so also we may ask those who have gone before us into eternity to pray for us.

If saints are our brothers and sisters in Christ and companions on our faith journey, then it makes sense to ask them to be patrons of particular causes. As patrons, we are asking various saints to take a special interest in something that may somehow have related to their lives on earth. This could be a cause, such as the pro-life movement; a group of people, such as parents of large families; or members of a profession, such as dentists or physicians. Churches and dioceses also have patrons, as well as some cities and countries.

St. Francis of Assisi, for example, encouraged his followers to honor and respect the natural world, so he is the patron saint of animals and those who work to protect the environment. He is also the patron of Assisi, Italy, and other cities. St. Francis de Sales was a writer, so he is the patron saint of journalists and writers. St. Clare of Assisi is the patron saint of television because one Christmas when she was too ill to attend Mass, she saw and heard Christmas Mass on her wall, even though it was happening in a different place.

At times popes have named saints as patrons of particular causes. After the conclusion of the First Vatican Council in 1870,

Pope Pius IX named St. Joseph, the husband of Mary, as patron of the universal Church. St. Joseph is also the patron of fathers and workers. Patrons also can be chosen by individuals, groups, or organizations. St. Isidore the Farmer is the patron saint of farmers and the United States National Rural Life Conference.

Popular saints such as Mary and St. Joseph are often selected as patrons of numerous causes. Each of the one hundred saints in this book has been identified with only one specific cause, but at times I have noted when a saint is also a patron of another group. Although it's often obvious why a saint is a patron of a particular cause, sometimes there seems to be no connection at all or only a peripheral one. For example, St. John Gualbert is the patron of forest workers because the first monastery he established was in a shady grove of trees.

The saints in this book span the two thousand years of Christianity. In the case of early Church saints, it's sometimes difficult to tell fact from fiction. We usually have good evidence that the saint existed and was martyred, but often legends developed around a particular saint, stories that both entertained and inspired people. Whatever really happened, however, we do know that these men and women were put to death for their belief in Jesus Christ. Their intercession is just as powerful as the saints whose lives we are more familiar with. At times the veneration and practices that followed the saints' deaths are as interesting as the lives of the saints themselves.

There are a few cases in which it's impossible to verify that a saint actually existed. St. Christopher is probably the best example of this situation. Then the Church tends to gently discourage devotion to him or her, although we can still be inspired and delight in these stories that are so much a part of our ancient tradition.

This book is arranged alphabetically by the cause to which a saint is attached. An index in the back of the book also lists the saints alphabetically by their first name so that you can easily find a particular saint. There are far more patron saints than those included in this book, of course, so you'll also find a list of resources for researching other patron saints.

As you read or browse through *The Patron Saints Handbook*, keep in mind that these saints were human just like all of us. Unlike us, however, they now enjoy what we experience only partially and imperfectly: loving intimacy with the God whom Dante in his *Divine Comedy* called "the Love that moves the sun and the other stars." Yet the very idea of patron saints takes for granted that the saints in heaven know what goes on in this world and in our lives, and they care for us and pray for us when we ask them to do so. How delightful is that!

Mitch Finley

1

Abuse Victims
Blessed Laura Vicuña
January 22

Laura Vicuña was born just three months after a civil war had erupted in Chile in 1891, so her life was in danger soon after it began. Claudio Vicuña, a relative of her father, was a prominent figure in the war—which left him with many enemies. The animosity toward him also threatened Laura and her family, and they moved to the Andean mountains for safety. In 1894 Laura's father died, leaving his wife, Mercedes, alone with her two daughters.

Mercedes became the mistress of a man named Manuel Mora in exchange for his protection and financial support. Mora sent Laura and her sister to a boarding school, which was run by the Salesian Sisters. Laura loved her new school—particularly the chapel that housed the tabernacle—and spent much of her time in prayer. At the age of ten, she made her First Holy Communion, which was a deeply spiritual experience for her. In her notebook at the time, she wrote, "O my God, I want to love you and serve you all my life. I give you my soul, my heart, my whole self." She asked the bishop who came to visit her school if she could become a Salesian Sister herself, but he responded that she was too young. Later, however, her confessor allowed her to take private vows.

Although she loved her time at school, Laura's life at home during school vacations was plagued with difficulties. Mora, who was often drunk, was becoming increasingly abusive and began making sexual advances toward the girl. Furthermore, Laura realized that her mother was neither happy nor close to God. This troubled her so much that she offered her life to God in exchange for her mother's salvation.

Laura fell ill in the winter of 1903 and returned home from school to recuperate and be with her mother. Mora's behavior grew steadily worse, and Laura and her family moved out. One night Mora caught up with them. He beat Laura until she was unconscious. She died several days later on January 22, 1904. After Laura's death, Mercedes returned to her faith and left Mora for good.

Laura was beatified by Pope John Paul II on September 3, 1988. Because she suffered and ultimately died at the hands of Mora, Laura is the patron saint of abuse victims. By dying she gave her mother the courage to escape a terrible domestic situation and to return to the Church. We may ask for her intercession to give us the strength to assert our rights in the face of abuse—physical or otherwise—as well as to deepen our faith.

2

ACTORS
St. Genesius
AUGUST 25

During the second and third centuries, Christians were frequently subjected to persecution by various Roman emperors. One of the most infamous of these emperors was Diocletian, who reigned from 284 until 305. When Diocletian first became emperor, he gave the impression that he might be more tolerant of Christianity than his predecessors, but this did not happen. For political reasons, Diocletian ordered that Christian churches be destroyed and that all copies of holy books be burned. He then denied all Christians in the empire their civil rights, which meant that they were no longer considered to be Roman citizens. Next, he directed that all members of the clergy be thrown in prison. All clergy who refused to offer sacrifice to the pagan gods were to be tortured and put to death. Before long he ordered that all Christians receive the same treatment.

Genesius was an actor who lived in Rome during the third century. One day he was performing in a play being presented for the emperor's entertainment. The play had been written to mock the Christian Sacrament of Baptism, and Genesius portrayed a catechumen who was to be baptized. While performing, however, Genesius underwent a conversion.

When Genesius' fellow actors took him before the emperor, Diocletian became enraged and sent him to Plautian, a high-ranking military officer. Plautian threatened him with torture if he didn't offer sacrifice to the pagan gods, but Genesius refused and insisted that he would be a Christian no matter what the cost. Genesius was then beheaded.

Certainly we can learn from the example of Genesius. We may not live in a society in which people are killed in huge numbers for being Christian, but in many countries in the world, acting on one's Christian faith can put a person in harm's way. In fact, notable individuals in the twentieth and twenty-first centuries have been murdered for precisely this reason. There is nothing out-of-date about the witness of Genesius.

Actors, whether amateur or professional, can learn from Genesius that it is important that there be no conflict between one's faith and one's art. They have a special gift, through which they may choose to influence people for good or for ill. Genesius, of course, would have them use it for the former.

3

ACCOUNTANTS
St. Matthew
SEPTEMBER 21

We learn about Matthew from the Gospels of Mark (2:14-17), Matthew (9:9-13), and Luke (5:27-32). Also known as Levi, Matthew was working as a tax collector in the town of Capernaum when Jesus called him. As a tax collector, Matthew was considered a public sinner, since tax collectors often extorted money from their fellow Jews. Despite this past, however, Jesus made Matthew one of his twelve apostles. Tradition teaches us that this is the same Matthew who authored the gospel that bears his name.

Just like the tax collectors of St. Matthew's time, in modern cultures accountants are sometimes viewed with scorn and disrespect. Consider the unkind term "bean counter," which is sometimes used to refer to accountants. The fact that tradition assigns an author of one of the four gospels to be the patron of accountants, however, should remind us that accounting can and should be a holy occupation.

Indeed, where would the Church be without accountants? From local parishes to the Vatican, the Church faces economic realities at every level and must be equipped to deal with them. There is no shortage of news stories about those who have given in to the temptation to be dishonest, but accountants can petition their patron saint, Matthew, to pray that they may carry out their duties with honesty and integrity. St. Matthew reminds us that anyone who manages and keeps track of money is called to do so in holy ways, whether they work for a huge corporation, a small business, or a local parish.

4

Altar Servers
St. John Berchmans
November 26

St. John Berchmans was born in 1599, the oldest son of a shoe-maker in the Brabant region of what is now Belgium. At the age of thirteen, he became a servant in the household of John Froymont, a cathedral canon at Malines. In 1615 he enrolled in the Jesuit college in Malines, and the next year he became a Jesuit novice. After three years at the college, he was sent to Rome to continue his studies. There he impressed everyone with his attention to detail, doing his best at even the most mundane tasks. He died while still a seminarian on August 13, 1621. Many miracles were attributed to him after his death, and he was canonized in 1888.

Today in most dioceses, altar servers can be either boys or girls. St. John Berchmans is the perfect patron for all who serve at the altar because this ministry requires attention to detail as well as reverence for the Eucharist and an understanding of the liturgical celebration. Even for young people who are not altar servers, this saint can be a model for their lives. John put effort into everything he did, from basic chores to his duties as a seminarian. He took his schooling seriously, and he gave serious thought and prayer to his state in life, finally deciding on a vocation as a priest. St. John is an inspiration for us to do our best always, whether it's performing small tasks or making big decisions, because it's all for the glory of God.

5

Animals
St. Francis of Assisi
October 4

*F*rancis of Assisi is one of the most popular saints in history, even outside the Catholic Church. Born in 1181, he was the son of a wealthy silk merchant and grew up much like any son of a rich man in those times, having anything he desired and dedicating his life to pleasure and fun.

In 1201 Francis joined the army of Assisi in fighting a war with nearby Perugia. He was taken prisoner, and after a year of captivity, he was released. He was on his way to another battle when he fell ill and heard God calling him to serve not man but the Lord. Over the next several years, Francis reflected on the state of his spiritual life. The turning point of his journey of faith was a chance meeting with a poor leper; when normally he would have been repulsed by the sight of such a person, Francis instead got off his horse, kissed the leper's hand, and gave him money. By 1208 Francis had discerned a calling to live in absolute poverty while preaching the word of God.

Eventually Francis gathered a few followers into a wandering community, and they became the first members of his Order of Friars Minor, commonly referred to as the Franciscans. Francis became known for his love of the natural world, especially animals. He preached sermons to birds and, according to one famous story, tamed a vicious wolf near the town of Gubbio. Francis often referred to animals as his brothers and sisters, and his famous "Canticle of the Sun" is a prayer of praise and thanksgiving for God's creation. Four years after his death in 1226, Francis was canonized.

Throughout the centuries, this saint has had a tremendous impact on the Church and on the faith and lives of Christians and others all over the world. He is often depicted preaching sermons to animals or birds, and backyard birdbaths with statues of St. Francis perched on them are an everyday reminder of his love for creation.

Many parishes have a blessing ritual for pets on October 4, the feast day of St. Francis. This practice reminds us of the Church's appreciation for all of God's creation, and in particular the animals that we welcome into our homes.

ARTHRITIS SUFFERERS
St. Alphonsus Liguori
AUGUST 1

St. Alphonsus was the founder of a religious community of missionary priests, a great moral theologian, and a doctor of the Church. In spite of these accomplishments, he faced opposition throughout his life. He also suffered from rheumatoid arthritis that was so severe that in the last twenty years of his life, his head was bent into his chest. This saint was well acquainted with suffering and therefore is the patron saint for those suffering from the pain and disability of arthritis.

Born on September 21, 1696, outside of Naples, Italy, Alphonsus was the son of a captain in the royal navy. He earned doctoral degrees in both canon and civil law from the University of Naples when he was only seventeen years old. For the next eight years, he conducted a successful law practice. However, when he lost an important case through an accidental oversight on his part, he gave up law and decided to become a priest. He was ordained in 1726. For the next two years, he served as a missionary in the vicinity of Naples. With his emphasis on God's mercy, Alphonsus became a sought-after confessor.

In 1730 Alphonsus was invited by the bishop of Castellammare to minister in his diocese. While giving a retreat to a group of nuns, he met Sr. Mary Celeste and became convinced that her vision of a new religious order was from God. This led to the founding of the Redemptorines. Later Alphonsus moved to Scala. There he organized the Congregation of the Most Holy Redeemer, or Redemptorists, a religious order dedicated to mission work. The rule of the congregation received papal approval in 1749 but lacked the approval of the king of Naples—a necessary step to ensure its continued existence.

In the meantime, Alphonsus became a prolific writer. His great work, *Moral Theology*, was a best seller during his lifetime. It emphasized not the rigid and legalistic spirituality of the time but the importance of a well-formed conscience so that Christians could use their freedom to make proper moral decisions and respond to God out of love.

At the age of sixty-six, Alphonsus was appointed bishop of a diocese near Naples and served tirelessly for thirteen years. He was permitted to retire at the age of eighty, but he lived for twelve more years, suffering from the physical pain of his arthritis as well as the pain of seeing his beloved rule changed drastically by the king of Naples. However, the order survived the squabbling and grew, and today Redemptorist missionaries serve throughout the world.

Alphonsus Liguori was canonized in 1839 and named a doctor of the Church in 1871. He is also the patron of confessors and moral theologians.

Artists
St. Catherine of Bologna
March 9

Catherine was born in Bologna, Italy, in 1413, the daughter of John de'Vigri, an attorney who was an aide to the marquis of Ferrara. At the age of eleven, the marquis asked that Catherine be allowed to live in his palace as maid of honor to his daughter, Margaret. The two girls, about the same age, became best friends. The friendship continued for several years. When Margaret became engaged to a nobleman, she wanted Catherine to remain her lady-in-waiting.

Catherine had several ardent suitors at the time, but she felt called to the religious life. At the age of fourteen, she joined a group of women who were lay Franciscans and who lived a quasi-monastic life. Eventually they adopted the Rule of the Poor Clares. When Catherine was asked to found a convent of Poor Clares in her home city of Bologna, she accepted and was abbess of that community from 1456 until her death in 1463.

Early in her life as a Poor Clare, Catherine began to have mystical experiences. For the edification of her community, she later talked about them. Her most widely known experience happened one Christmas Eve. She had asked permission to be alone in the convent chapel that evening. She planned to recite one thousand Hail Marys in honor of the birth of Christ. At midnight the Blessed Mother appeared to Catherine with the infant Jesus in her arms. Mary gave the child to Catherine, who held him close and kissed him on the cheek. When she tried to kiss him on the lips, he disappeared, but Catherine said she continued to feel a deep sense of joy.

Like most true mystics, Catherine was grounded in the real world; she had considerable talent and abundant common sense. She was a gifted artist and undertook the task of copying by hand all the prayers in her prayer book and illustrating the texts with small, colorful images of Jesus, Mary, and the saints. She also painted large religious pictures, composed sacred music, and wrote several devotional books.

Catherine was in poor health for many years and died on March 9, 1463. Not long after her death, many who prayed for her intercession experienced miraculous cures. She was canonized in 1712.

Because she was a talented artist, Catherine is the patron saint of artists. She teaches us that we should never underestimate the value of art and the ways in which it can nourish the spiritual life. The Church has been a patron of the arts for many centuries, and artists have contributed to the life of the Church in all eras.

8

ASTRONAUTS AND AVIATORS
St. Joseph of Cupertino
SEPTEMBER 18

Joseph (Giuseppe) Desa was born to poor parents in Cupertino, Italy, in 1603. He had an unhappy childhood; after his father died, Joseph's mother viewed him as a burden and treated him abusively. He was apprenticed to a shoemaker but could not learn the trade, and the people of his village thought that he was mentally disabled.

Although he had a hot temper, Joseph was exceptionally devout. After being rejected by two different Franciscan communities, he was finally accepted by the Conventual Franciscans in Grottela. He struggled with his studies but was ordained a priest in 1628. Soon Joseph became famous for his various religious ecstasies and miracles, and in particular for his frequent levitations. Indeed, he came to be known as "the flying friar," and this seems to be why he was named the patron saint of astronauts, aviators, and air travelers. It was recorded that Joseph levitated on seventy different occasions at Grotella during his seventeen years there.

Joseph's levitations attracted outside attention, causing much consternation among the monks, and his superiors forbade him to say Mass in public, attend choir, participate in processions, or eat with the community in the friary dining room. In 1639 Fr. Joseph was transferred to Assisi, where he lived for thirteen years. In 1653 Joseph was again moved, this time to a more remote friary. Eventually people discovered where he was living and sought him out for spiritual counsel and prayer. Because of this unwanted attention, he was sent to the friars' community in Ossimo. On September 18, 1663, Joseph died in Ossimo and was buried there.

People began visiting Joseph's burial place almost immediately, and many healing miracles took place at his tomb. He was beatified in 1753 and canonized in 1767. Joseph was made a saint not for his numerous levitations but for being so patient, gentle, and humble. Even though he was ostracized within his own community and shuttled from one friary to another, Joseph displayed willing obedience. We can learn from St. Joseph of Cupertino to persevere in our faith and always be kind and obedient, even when we are rejected by others.

ASTRONOMERS
St. Dominic
AUGUST 8

St. Dominic was born in 1170 in Caleruega in the Castile region of Spain. His father, Felix de Guzman, was the warden of the town, and his mother, Joan, was later beatified. According to one famous story, when his mother was pregnant with Dominic, she had a dream in which she gave birth to a dog. The dog ran away from her carrying a burning torch in its mouth, with which it would set the world on fire. This dog became a symbol of the religious order Dominic founded, and later it gave rise to a nickname for those who belonged to the order: "the watchdogs of the Lord."

When Dominic was seven years old, he was sent to live with his uncle, a parish priest. He studied the arts and theology. While still a student, he was made a canon of the cathedral of Osma. After he was ordained a priest, he lived under the rule of St. Augustine and had a reputation for a deep spirituality. For a number of years he lived a contemplative life.

In 1201, when he was thirty-one years old, he was chosen to accompany the bishop of Osma on a journey to Denmark, where the bishop was to negotiate a marriage for the son of King Alfonso IX of Castile. Passing through Languedoc in southern France, the bishop and Dominic stayed one night in the home of a man who had embraced the Albigensian heresy. This heresy taught that the material world is evil and thus rejected the Incarnation.

Dominic felt deep compassion for this man and spent the night in conversation with him. At daybreak the man realized his error and embraced the true Christian faith. From this time on, Dominic knew that he was called by God to teach and call those in error to the truth. He spent the next ten years as a preacher against Albigensianism, teaching the goodness of creation and the truth of God becoming man in Jesus Christ. A small band of followers joined him to preach the same message. In 1216 this small community began living together as the Order of Preachers, which later became known as the Dominicans. Later that year Pope Honorius III approved Dominic's order and the rule of life that he had written.

Dominic emphasized the importance of academic study as preparation for effective preaching, but he placed the greatest emphasis on the need for each member of the order to cultivate personal holiness. During the remaining years of his life, Dominic traveled extensively and preached the gospel wherever he went. He died in 1221 and was canonized in 1234. He is the patron saint of astronomers because of his dedication to scholarship and to preaching the goodness of God's creation.

ATHLETES
St. Sebastian
JANUARY 20

Much of what we know about St. Sebastian comes from the writings of St. Ambrose. While some of the story may be pious legend, we know for sure that Sebastian was martyred for his Christian faith about the year 288, that he was buried near Rome on the Appian Way, and that he was venerated in Milan, Italy.

St. Ambrose tells us that Sebastian was born in the city of Narbonne on the southern coast of what is now France. He was a fervent Christian. Although he was not inclined to military life, around the year 283 he became a Roman soldier in order to help persecuted Christians. His military position also gave him an opportunity to evangelize various prominent Roman citizens.

In 286 the persecution of Christians had reached a fever pitch, and several close Christian friends of Sebastian were tortured and killed. When the emperor Diocletian discovered that Sebastian was a Christian as well, he ordered some archers to shoot him with arrows until he died. When Irene, the wife of one of Sebastian's martyred friends, went to retrieve his body for burial, she discovered that he was still alive. Nursed back to health by Irene, Sebastian refused to escape. Instead, one day he waited in a spot where he knew the emperor was to pass by, and when the emperor appeared, Sebastian stood before Diocletian and denounced his persecution of Christians.

Diocletian had thought that Sebastian was dead, so initially he was taken aback by Sebastian's presence and words. Recovering from his shock, however, the emperor ordered that Sebastian be taken prisoner and beaten to death and that his body be thrown into a sewer. After Sebastian's death, a woman named Lucina had a vision of Sebastian, and she arranged for his body to be secretly buried in a place near the Appian Way. Later a basilica was constructed on the site of Sebastian's grave, possibly by the emperor Constantine in the early fourth century.

Sebastian is often portrayed in pious art still alive, with numerous arrows piercing his body. He is the patron of athletes because he underwent such intense physical ordeals for the sake of his faith.

11

AUTHORS
St. Francis de Sales
JANUARY 24

*F*rancis de Sales is one of the great saints of the Church. His writings and preaching encouraged holiness among laypeople, a revolutionary idea in his time. He was born on August 21, 1567, into a prominent family in Savoy, France. He was well educated and received a doctorate in law at the age of twenty-four from the University of Padua, where he also studied theology. Even though his family initially opposed his plan, Francis chose to study for the priesthood and was ordained in 1593. He spent the next five years as a missionary in the Chablais region of France, working to convert Calvinists back to the Church.

Francis succeeded in attracting thousands of people in the region back to Catholicism, not by force, but through logic and appeals to the heart. He was named the bishop of Geneva in 1602 and was soon widely recognized as a great preacher, pastor, and theologian. He established schools, instructed countless people in the faith, and governed his diocese with both wisdom and practical insight. In 1604 he met Jane Frances de Chantal and became her spiritual adviser. Together in 1610 they founded a religious order for women, the Order of the Visitation.

Francis de Sales died in Lyons, France, on December 28, 1622. Two of the books he wrote were popular in his day and have become spiritual classics: *Introduction to the Devout Life* and

Treatise on the Love of God. Both emphasize the idea that holiness is possible through the many opportunities that God gives us in our ordinary lives. Francis also stressed this theme in his many letters of spiritual direction. He was canonized in 1665 and named a doctor of the Church in 1877—an honor that recognizes the recipient as a major theological influence whose writings are recommended for their wisdom and orthodoxy.

Authors today can take Francis de Sales as an inspiration when it comes to blending the work of writing with their personal faith and spirituality. Francis was a man of prayer and a writer who saw his gift as a vocation from God.

12

BAKERS
St. Elizabeth of Hungary
NOVEMBER 17

*B*orn in 1207, Elizabeth was the daughter of King Andrew II of Hungary. When she was four years old, Elizabeth was promised in marriage to Ludwig, the son of the Duke of Thuringia. When Elizabeth was fourteen and Ludwig was twenty-one, the couple married, and Elizabeth gave birth to two children.

Elizabeth became widely known for her dedication to caring for the poor, personally visiting the sick and feeding hundreds of people each day. She even built a hospital at the foot of her castle. According to one story, as she was secretly going on an errand of mercy, she unexpectedly met Ludwig. The basket of bread that she was carrying changed miraculously into a basket of roses.

After departing to participate in a crusade in 1227, Ludwig died, and Elizabeth gave birth to their third child. When she received the news of his death, Elizabeth mourned deeply. She then became a Third Order Franciscan, built a Franciscan hospital in Marburg, and renounced all her worldly possessions.

Elizabeth died on November 17, 1231, at the age of twenty-four. She was canonized in 1253, and in 1236 her remains were taken to the newly built church of St. Elizabeth in Marburg. This church became a popular pilgrimage site until the Duke of Hesse, a Lutheran, ordered that Elizabeth's relics be moved elsewhere. To this day no one knows where they are. Even so, visitors to

Marburg today find that St. Elizabeth of Hungary still has an important spiritual presence there.

St. Elizabeth of Hungary was chosen as the patron saint of bakers because of her charitable distribution of bread and other food to the poor. Her life is a reminder of the need to share what we have with those who have less.

13

Bicyclists
Madonna del Ghisallo
October 13

Madonna del Ghisallo is one of the many honorary titles for the Blessed Virgin Mary, although one that is not widely known. Pope Pius XII declared the Madonna of Ghisallo the patron saint of cyclists during the 1949 Giro d'Italia, a long-distance bicycle race in Italy for professional cyclists that is held each year in May or June.

According to legend, a medieval count named Ghisallo was under attack from thieves when he saw an image of the Virgin Mary at a nearby shrine. Running toward the shrine, he was saved from the robbers. The apparition became known as the Madonna del Ghisallo, and she became a patron saint of travelers in the region.

In 1949 a local priest, Fr. Ermelindo Vigano, proposed that Madonna del Ghisallo be declared the patron saint of cyclists, and Pope Pius XII agreed. Today the shrine of Madonna del Ghisallo includes a small museum on the sport of cycling with photos and souvenirs from the Giro d'Italia. The shrine also houses an eternal flame in memory of cyclists who have died. A particularly important artifact is the wrecked bicycle ridden by Fabio Casartelli, a native of the region, who died in a crash in the world-famous Tour de France on July 18, 1995.

Some of the greatest riders in the world have given their bicycles and jerseys to the shrine as an act of thanksgiving for winning races. Many people make a visit to the tiny church, which is the centerpiece of the shrine. Some cyclists feel that the only appropriate way to get to the chapel is by bicycle, and they make the ride a kind of pilgrimage. While there is a parking lot for cars at the chapel, the bicycle racks nearby are used far more often. Many cyclists attest to the powerful feelings associated with a visit to the chapel.

For bicyclists, the most popular souvenir at the shrine is a small holy medal bearing the image of Madonna del Ghisallo. Many professional bicyclists wind the medal's chain on their bicycle frame. The idea behind using the medal is to externalize one's faith in God's protection through prayer to the Blessed Mother under her title of Madonna del Ghisallo.

14

Blood Banks
St. Januarius
September 19

J anuarius was the bishop of Naples during the vicious persecution of Christians launched by the emperor Diocletian in 303.
When Januarius learned that his deacon and friend, Sossius, had
been imprisoned along with two other Christians, he went to
visit them. Upon his arrival at the prison, Januarius and his two
companions were also taken captive. Then they were put into an
enclosed space with wild beasts. When the animals did not harm
them, Januarius and the others were taken out and beheaded.

At some point in the fifth century, Januarius' relics were trans-
ported to Naples, then moved to various locations, and in 1497
were returned to the cathedral in Naples. Ever since then, a vial
said to contain the blood of St. Januarius, which appears as a
dark, solid, and opaque substance, is kept in a special chapel in
the cathedral. On three different feast days each year, the vial
is brought out and held up for the veneration of the faithful.
A group of women called the *Zie di San Gennaro* (Aunts of St.
Januarius) leads the assembly in prayers. As they do so, the substance in the vial begins to liquefy and turn dark red. On some
occasions, the liquefied substance also bubbles as if boiling. A
priest announces to the assembly, "The miracle has happened,"
at which everyone sings the *Te Deum*, a traditional Latin hymn
of praise and thanksgiving to God.

Modern science has neither proven nor disproven the authenticity of this phenomenon. Nonetheless, anyone who has ever benefitted from a blood transfusion knows the value of the gift of blood given by someone else, often an anonymous stranger. It makes perfect sense to pray for the intercession of St. Januarius on behalf of blood banks, those who donate blood, and those who receive this often lifesaving gift.

15

BODILY ILLS
St. Bernadette Soubirous
APRIL 16

The Shrine of Our Lady of Lourdes in southwestern France is the most popular Christian pilgrimage site in the world. People travel there to seek the healing properties of the spring waters that appeared in 1858 during apparitions of the Blessed Virgin Mary to a destitute girl of fourteen named Bernadette Soubirous.

Bernadette was the daughter of a poor miller in Lourdes. An undersized girl who suffered from asthma and had not yet made her first Communion, Bernadette saw a vision one day in February as she was going to gather firewood with her sister and a friend. The young and beautiful lady who appeared to her in the hollow of a rock was "lovelier than I have ever seen," Bernadette said. The woman was clothed in white with a blue ribbon sash and a rosary hanging from her right arm.

One day the apparition told the girl to drink from a spring in the grotto. Even though there was no indication of water, Bernadette dug at the ground with her hands, and spring water bubbled up. Another time the apparition asked Bernadette to tell the parish priest that she wanted a chapel to be built by the springs. She also asked that processions be made to the grotto. Mary appeared to Bernadette a total of eighteen times, from February through July.

The parish priest was skeptical and urged Bernadette to find out the lady's name. After the next apparition, Bernadette told the priest that the lady had told her, "I am the Immaculate Conception." The girl had never heard the term before, but just four years earlier, the pope had established the doctrine of the Immaculate Conception of the Virgin Mary.

Four years after Bernadette's visions, in 1862, the local bishop announced that the faithful were "justified in believing the reality of the apparition" of Our Lady, and as she had requested, a basilica was built in the spot where she appeared. Several years later a larger basilica was built in Lourdes to accommodate the crowds. Over the years, many miraculous healings have taken place in Lourdes, both physical and spiritual.

Bernadette was interrogated intensely but never wavered in her accounts of the apparitions. Later she went to a school run by the Sisters of Charity, where she learned to read and write. At the age of twenty-two, she joined the Sisters of Charity and moved into their motherhouse at Nevers. Bernadette spent the rest of her life in this convent, working as an assistant in the infirmary and later as a sacristan. In her early thirties, she contracted tuberculosis, and on April 16, 1879, at the age of thirty-five, she died. Because of the numerous healings at Lourdes and her own bodily suffering, Bernadette is the patron saint for those with bodily ills.

Over the years more than seven thousand pilgrims have claimed to have been healed after bathing in or drinking Lourdes water. The Church has officially declared sixty-seven cures to be authentic miracles, the latest in 2005.

Booksellers
St. John of God
March 8

St. John of God is one of Spain's leading religious figures. He was born in Montemoro Novo, Portugal, on March 8, 1495, into a deeply religious family that was poor but had once been wealthy and prominent. As a young man, John worked for a farmer as a shepherd. The farmer, pleased with how strong and diligent John was, offered him his daughter's hand in marriage to ensure that John would become the farmer's heir. John declined, however, and moved to Spain.

In Spain he served heroically as a soldier under the holy Roman emperor Charles V. Then he worked in Granada as a peddler of holy pictures and religious books. He also produced books himself using the recently developed Gutenberg moveable-type printing press. His patronage of booksellers stems from this period in his life.

John underwent a major religious conversion on St. Sebastian's Day (January 20) while listening to a sermon by St. John of Ávila, the man who later became his spiritual guide. About this time, John had a mental breakdown and was confined to an institution. In 1539, with the help of John of Ávila, he recovered. The experience convinced him that the poor deserved better treatment. He dedicated the rest of his life to caring for the needy.

John gradually attracted a group of dedicated men who felt called to join him in this ministry. Donations from the wealthy who admired his holiness and dedication made it possible for John to continue his work. He organized his disciples into what he called the Order of Hospitallers, now known as the Hospitaller Brothers of St. John of God. This religious order cares for the sick in many countries around the world. These men are also officially entrusted with the medical care of the pope.

John died on March 8, 1550, which was his fifty-fifth birthday. In 1690 he was canonized by Pope Alexander VIII.

BRICKLAYERS
St. Stephen of Hungary
AUGUST 16

St. Stephen is considered the founder of an independent Hungary and was its first Christian king. He was born in 975, the son of the ruler of the Magyars, an ethnic group in Hungary. He was baptized a Christian in 985 at the same time as his father. At age twenty, he married Gisela, the sister of Duke Henry III of Bavaria, and when his father died in 977, Stephen succeeded him.

Stephen had to fight a series of wars with rival leaders, but soon he united the country and established Christianity as the religion of Hungary. On Christmas Day 1001, Emperor Otto III crowned Stephen the first king of Hungary, using a crown sent to him by Pope Sylvester II. This famous crown was centuries later captured during World War II by the U.S. Army. It was returned to Hungary in 1978.

Stephen established a church hierarchy in Hungary. He set up dioceses, built churches, and arranged for a system of tithes to support this work. He later completed the building of St. Martin's Monastery, which his father had started. Stephen carried out widespread civil reforms, including a new legal code and the reorganization of the government. He ruled with wisdom and generosity.

Stephen died at Szekesfehervar, Hungary, on August 15, 1038. Miracles were attributed to him at his tomb, and in 1083 he was canonized by Pope Gregory VII. His relics were placed in a shrine in the Church of Our Lady in Budapest. In 2000 Bartholomew I of Constantinople, the ecumenical patriarch, recognized Stephen as a saint in the Orthodox Church. In Hungary St. Stephen has always been considered a national hero and the most important of the country's Christian kings.

Stephen is the patron saint of bricklayers as well as stonecutters and masons. While there is no direct connection to Stephen and this trade, he was responsible for the building of churches throughout Hungary.

18

Broadcasters
St. Gabriel the Archangel
September 29

*I*n Hebrew the name Gabriel means "man of God." In an apostolic letter dated January 21, 1951, Pope Pius XII declared that St. Gabriel the Archangel is the patron saint of broadcasters and all who work in the telecommunications industry. That's because in the Scriptures, Gabriel is the heavenly messenger who brings to humankind messages from God, such as in this passage from the Old Testament Book of Daniel:

> When I, Daniel, had seen the vision, I tried to understand it. Then someone appeared standing before me, having the appearance of a man, and I heard a human voice by the Ulai, calling, "Gabriel, help this man understand the vision." So he came near where I stood; and when he came, I became frightened and fell prostrate. But he said to me, "Understand, O mortal, that the vision is for the time of the end."
>
> As he was speaking to me, I fell into a trance, face to the ground; then he touched me and set me on my feet. He said, "Listen, and I will tell you what will take place later in the period of wrath." (Daniel 8:15-19)

In the Gospel of Luke, God sends Gabriel to announce the birth of John the Baptist to Zechariah: "The angel replied, 'I am

Gabriel. I stand in the presence of God, and I have been sent to speak to you and to bring you this good news'" (1:19).

Also in Luke's Gospel, Gabriel is the one who announces to Mary the conception of Jesus: "In the sixth month the angel Gabriel was sent by God to a town in Galilee called Nazareth, to a virgin engaged to a man whose name was Joseph, of the house of David. The virgin's name was Mary" (1:26-27). The annunciation is, in fact, the subject of a fifth-century mosaic in the Basilica of St. Mary Major in Rome, which is the oldest known portrayal of an angel with feet and wings.

Scholars have traced devotion to St. Gabriel the Archangel to the earliest days of Christianity in Rome. In the tradition of the early Christians, Gabriel was said to have guarded the Tree of Life and was also the angel who expelled Adam and Eve from Eden.

The angel Gabriel is often pictured holding a scroll bearing the words of the Hail Mary.

19

BUILDERS
St. Vincent Ferrer
APRIL 5

St. Vincent Ferrer was a Spanish Dominican priest and a powerful preacher who attracted large crowds throughout Europe. So popular was he that often a church couldn't accommodate all the people who came to hear him, and he had to preach outdoors instead.

Born in Valencia, Spain, in 1350, Vincent was ordained sometime between 1374 and 1379. While living in Barcelona, he gained considerable attention when, during a famine, he accurately predicted the arrival of ships loaded with grain.

The life and ministry of Vincent Ferrer coincided with a major division in the Western Church, which resulted in two different men being elected as pope, one of whom lived in Avignon, France. Vincent supported the Avignon popes. In 1394, when his friend, Cardinal Peter de Luna, became Benedict XIII, Vincent moved to Avignon and was given prominent roles to fill, including serving as the pope's personal theologian.

During a French siege of Avignon, Vincent became seriously ill and almost died. When he recovered, he declared it a miracle because it had occurred after he had a vision of Jesus, St. Dominic, and St. Francis of Assisi. In his vision he was instructed to preach far and wide. However, the pope was reluctant to let Vincent leave Avignon. He finally relented and allowed Vincent to depart for a preaching tour throughout Western Europe. Hundreds of miraculous healings occurred when Vincent preached.

In time and in spite of his belief that Benedict XIII was the legitimate pope, Vincent saw how much harm the schism had caused. In great part through his efforts, the schism ended. Vincent became a kind of apostle of church unity, traveling extensively to preach on this theme.

Vincent Ferrer died on April 5, 1419, in Vannes, in the Brittany region of France. He was canonized by Pope Callistus III in 1455. While this saint did not physically build houses or churches, he did build unity in the Church—a great achievement for which he will be long remembered. He also strengthened the Church through his preaching and missionary travels.

BUS DRIVERS
St. Christopher
JULY 25

Christopher is said to have lived in Asia Minor—modern day Turkey—during the third century and died about the year 250. Little is known about Christopher, and the historical value of what we do know is questionable. Some scholars say that he was a martyr known originally as Kester. According to the legend, Christopher was an unattractive, very large man who used his size to his advantage. He made his living by carrying people across a river that had no bridge.

One day a small boy asked to be carried to the other side. Christopher put the little boy on his shoulder and walked into the river, but with each step the child grew heavier. Fearing for his own safety, Christopher struggled against the river's currents. At this point the boy revealed that he was the Christ Child, and the reason he was so heavy was because he bore the weight of the world. Thus "Christopher" means "Christ bearer."

Relics said to be those of Christopher are kept in both Rome and Paris. Originally Christopher was the patron saint of ferry workers. This role expanded to include travelers, and in the twentieth century, bus drivers and those traveling by automobile. Medals of St. Christopher are popular; they are often worn on a chain around the neck, kept on key rings, or displayed in automobiles, buses, airplanes, boats, and other vehicles.

Even though St. Christopher is no longer on the Church's official calendar and his existence is in doubt, his name continues to appear on lists of patron saints as the patron of bus drivers and of motor vehicle drivers.

That may be because the story of St. Christopher holds powerful sway over the popular imagination. We pray to historical saints, not because they have some power independent of the power of God, but because we want their companionship and prayers as we turn to our loving Father with our needs and concerns. When people pray to St. Christopher, they are essentially turning to God in the company of a delightful story. To pray to St. Christopher is to say to God, "Here I am, praying for a safe journey for those I love and for myself, and by the way, Lord, here is this wonderful story, which is a prayer in itself. Amen."

BUSINESS MEN AND WOMEN
St. Homobonus
NOVEMBER 13

Omobono Tucenghi, known as St. Homobonus, was born late in the twelfth century. He certainly lived up to his name, which comes from the Latin words *homo* and *bonus*, meaning "good man." Taught the merchant business in Cremona, Italy, by his father, Homobonus was a prosperous tailor and merchant. He was married and lived a good life, conducting his business with the utmost honesty and integrity. He was known for his generosity and charity to the poor, and believed that God wanted him to use his profits to help people who were living in poverty.

A daily communicant, Homobonus went to Mass on November 13, 1197, in Cremona, and after prostrating himself in the form of a cross, he died. Two years later Homobonus was canonized by Pope Innocent III. During the canonization liturgy, the pope called Homobonus "father of the poor" and a peacemaker who consoled the afflicted and prayed constantly.

In a letter to the bishop of Cremona in 1997, Pope John Paul II said of this saint, "Homobonus' image emerges as that of a businessman engaged in the cloth trade and, while involved in the market dynamics of Italian and European cities, conferred spiritual dignity on his work: that spirituality which was the hallmark of all his activity."

Homobonus' generosity with the money he earned makes him an ideal patron saint for business men and women. The church of Sant'Omobono in Rome is dedicated to him.

22

BUTCHERS
St. Anthony of Egypt
JANUARY 17

*B*orn in Egypt about 251, Anthony was one of the founders of Christian monasticism. We know about his life because of a famous biography written of him by St. Athanasius, which helped fuel the spread of monasticism, especially in the West.

Anthony wanted to live like the early disciples and leave all behind for Christ. Following the death of his wealthy parents, he placed his sister in a convent—not an unusual practice at the time—and sold all he owned. He gave the money to the poor and at the age of twenty moved into an empty hut to live as a hermit.

However, desiring even more solitude, at the age of thirty-five Anthony moved alone to the desert, living for the next twenty years in an abandoned fort. St. Athanasius relates many stories of Anthony's battles with the devil during this time, even to the point of death. Anthony ate only bread and water, which was often given to him by admirers who threw the food over the wall of the fort.

Eventually admirers broke into the old fort. Anthony miraculously healed sick people and gave spiritual advice. Gradually word about Anthony spread, and so many disciples arrived that a community of monks formed on the Nile at Pispir. For five or six years, Anthony instructed the monks but then felt called to withdraw even farther into the desert. He settled on a mountain, where he spent the last forty-five years of his life. Although he lived in seclusion, he did see those who came to visit him, and at times he also crossed the desert to visit Pispir.

Twice in his life, Anthony went to Alexandria: once in 311 to comfort those persecuted by the Roman emperor Maximinus, and again in 350 to combat the Arian heresy. Anthony died around 356 at the age of 105 without ever becoming ill. When he died, two of his disciples buried Anthony's body, according to his directions, beside his cell.

Why is St. Anthony associated with pigs and butchers? In Anthony's time, diseases of the skin were sometimes treated with applications of pork fat to reduce inflammation and irritation. Since Anthony's prayerful intervention helped with the same skin conditions, he was later shown in art accompanied by a pig. People who saw the artwork thought that there was a direct connection between Anthony, pigs, and, by extension, butchering.

23

CAB DRIVERS
St. Fiacre
SEPTEMBER I

*F*iacre was probably born in Ireland around the year 670. As a young man, he sailed to France in search of greater solitude so that he could devote himself more completely to God. He went to Meaux in northern France, and the local bishop, Faro, gave Fiacre a secluded place to live in a forest called Breuil, which Faro had inherited. According to legend, Faro told Fiacre that he could have as much land as he could plow up in one day. Instead of using a plow, Fiacre turned up the soil with the point of his staff, thus obtaining far more land than he would have otherwise.

St. Fiacre cleared the land of trees and shrubs and built a small hut with a garden. He also built another small hut, which he dedicated to the Blessed Virgin and used only for prayer. In addition, he built a hospice for travelers, which eventually became the village of Saint-Fiacre in the Seine-et-Marne region. Many people went to St. Fiacre for spiritual guidance, and he cheerfully helped the poor who came to him for assistance. Indeed, Fiacre came to be known widely for his many miracles of healing.

A man of his times, Fiacre wouldn't allow women near his hermitage, nor would he allow women to enter his chapel. Anne of Austria, who was Queen of France at the time, often remained outside Fiacre's chapel to pray among the ordinary pilgrims.

The date of St. Fiacre's death is unknown, but after his death, the shrine that was established at his hermitage became famous for the healing miracles that continued to take place there. People visited the shrine for centuries afterward. Members of the royalty and the Church's hierarchy also testified to the efficacy of the intercession of St. Fiacre. The bodily remains of St. Fiacre are located at Meaux, and people still go there to pray for his intercession regarding all sorts of physical ailments.

St. Fiacre became the patron saint of the cab drivers of Paris in the mid-seventeenth century. French cabs are called fiacres because the first business to have cabs for hire was in the Rue St.-Martin, which is close to the Hôtel St.-Fiacre in Paris. Later St. Fiacre was adopted as a patron by cab drivers in other countries as well.

24

CANCER PATIENTS
St. Peregrine Laziosi
MAY 1

Peregrine Laziosi was born to wealthy parents in 1260 at Forli in the Romagna region of Italy. As a young man, he participated actively in local politics and belonged to a party that opposed the pope. However, in the midst of a protest demonstration, something happened that changed his life. The pope had sent the future saint, Philip Benizi, to act as mediator, and Philip was handled roughly by the leaders of the protest. Peregrine struck Philip in the face, but Philip's only response was to turn his head so Peregrine could hit him again. This response touched Peregrine deeply, and he experienced a profound conversion.

Peregrine stopped associating with his former companions and spent time in prayer in the chapel of the Blessed Virgin Mary in Forli's cathedral. Mary appeared to Peregrine and instructed him to go to Siena and join the Servite Order, which he did. There he was ordained a priest. It was said that one of the penances he imposed on himself was to remain standing whenever he had the opportunity to sit.

After some years, his superiors sent Peregrine back to Forli to found a new community for the order. Not long after returning, Peregrine developed cancer in his foot, which caused extreme pain and made it very unpleasant for others to be around him. Eventually the doctors decided to amputate. The night before the surgery was scheduled, Peregrine remained awake and at prayer before a crucifix. Then he fell asleep and had a vision of Christ leaving the cross and touching his foot. When he woke up, his cancerous foot had been healed completely. The doctors were amazed and declared that they could find no trace of the cancer. This miracle increased Peregrine's reputation as a man of God. He died in 1345 at the age of eighty and was canonized in 1726.

Given the prevalence of cancer today, St. Peregrine is a popular saint. Many pray novenas to him to be healed of cancer and wear St. Peregrine medals so that they can have a visual reminder of God's care of them. The National Shrine of St. Peregrine in Chicago holds a Mass for the Sick with the relics of the saint once a month.

CATECHISTS
St. Charles Borromeo
NOVEMBER 4

St. Charles Borromeo was one of the most important and influential bishops in the history of the Church. Instead of leaving the Church because of the corruption that had in part led to the Protestant Reformation, he became a major catalyst for change and renewal during the Catholic Counter-Reformation.

Charles was born October 2, 1538, into a wealthy and aristocratic Italian family that owned a castle on Lake Maggiore. In 1559 Charles' uncle became Pope Pius IV, and Charles, a layman, became the new pope's secretary of state. He enthusiastically supported his uncle's decision to reconvene the Council of Trent in 1562. (The council had been in recess due to various wars and plagues since 1552.) Charles participated actively in the writing of the Catechism of the Council of Trent and in the reform of Church music and various liturgical books.

In 1563 Charles was ordained a priest, and only two months later was made a bishop. As the pope's representative for the entire country of Italy, Charles convened a provincial council in Milan to introduce the reforms of the Council of Trent.

When his uncle died, Charles received permission from the new pope, Pius V, to reside in his diocese, thus becoming the first resident archbishop of Milan in some eighty years. Adopting a very simple lifestyle, Charles gave much of his income to the poor. He reformed the administration of the archdiocese, visited parishes regularly, set up seminaries, established and enforced standards of ethical behavior for the clergy, and founded a society to teach the basics of the faith to children.

Charles' efforts to reform the Church were not always well received. In 1569 a priest who belonged to a rebellious order tried to kill Charles. Fortunately Charles was only slightly wounded, and the group was suppressed.

Charles died in Milan on November 3, 1584, at the age of forty-eight and was buried in the cathedral there. He was canonized in 1610. Blessed John XXIII, who was also involved in Church reforms, had a special devotion to St. Charles Borromeo and studied his life over several decades.

Charles was named patron of catechists because of his personal dedication to catechesis and because he founded a society to support, educate, and encourage catechists. Charles Borromeo knew the importance of catechesis in the life and faith of the Church, and catechists today can trust in this bishop for his prayers and support.

26

Charitable Societies
St. Vincent de Paul
September 27

St. Vincent de Paul—his name has become synonymous with charity—was born into a French peasant family on April 24, 1581. He attended the college in Dax and later the University of Toulouse, and was ordained a priest in 1600 at the young age of nineteen. In 1605 he was returning from Marseilles—where he had gone to collect a legacy that had been left to him—and was captured by pirates and sold as a slave in Tunisia. Two years later he managed to escape and went to Avignon, and from there to Rome for further studies.

In 1612 Vincent became a tutor in the household of the Count de Gondi, an aristocrat, which enabled him to meet wealthy people who would later fund his charitable work. With the help of Madame de Gondi, he began preaching missions to the peasants on her estate. So many people were moved by his words that Vincent had to call in more priests to hear confessions. In 1619 he became chaplain to the convicts in the galleys, and many were converted by his kind words and his efforts to relieve their physical suffering.

In 1625 Vincent founded the Congregation of the Mission, later also known as the Vincentians, which was dedicated to missionary work among the peasants. He also established parish confraternities to serve the poor, and in 1633 he joined St. Louise de Marillac to found the Daughters of Charity. He built hospitals and orphanages, ransomed Christian slaves in the north of Africa, helped improve the education of priests by establishing new seminaries, sent his priests on missionary journeys, and wrote on many spiritual topics.

St. Vincent de Paul's whole life was devoted to bringing relief to those who were poor and afflicted. He died in Paris on September 27, 1660, and was canonized by Pope Clement XII in 1737. In 1885 Pope Leo XIII declared St. Vincent de Paul the patron saint of all charitable organizations.

More than four hundred biographies have been written about Vincent, and a 1947 movie, *Monsieur Vincent,* was made about his life. Chapters of the St. Vincent de Paul Society serve the poor in parishes all over the world. Through his intercession, may we also be inspired to be generous with our time and treasure.

CHASTITY
St. Thomas Aquinas
JANUARY 28

St. Thomas Aquinas, one of the greatest theologians in the history of the Church, was born about 1225 in Sicily. His father, Count Landulf of Aquino, was related to the emperor and also to the king of France. When Thomas was five years old, he was sent to the Benedictine monastery of Monte Cassino to be educated. Starting in about 1239, he attended the University of Naples, and in 1244 he chose to enter the Order of Preachers, also known as the Dominicans. His parents were so opposed to this decision that they had Thomas kidnapped and held prisoner at Roccasecca Castle in an attempt to change his mind. Thomas was determined, however, and rejoined the Dominicans in 1245, studying at the University of Paris from 1245 to 1248.

In 1248 he went with Albert the Great—another great Dominican theologian—to a new Dominican house of studies in Cologne, and he was ordained a priest. In 1252 he returned to Paris as a theology teacher. Twenty years later, he was appointed to head up a new Dominican house of studies in Naples. He was en route to attend the General Council of Lyons, which was convened in order to discuss the reunion of the Greek and Latin churches, when he died on March 7, 1274. He was canonized by Pope John XXII in 1323 and was declared a doctor of the Church by Pope St. Pius V in 1567.

Thomas wrote prolifically, and among his many works he is most famous for his *Summa Theologica*, a systematic statement of all Christian doctrine. He believed that truth is known by both reason and faith. A year before his death, however, he had an intense experience of God at Mass, which led him to say, "All I have written seems like straw to me."

Thomas Aquinas is the patron saint of theologians, but why is he also patron of the virtue of chastity? During his imprisonment, when his family was trying to dissuade him from joining the Dominicans, two of Thomas' brothers sent a prostitute into his cell to seduce him. When he saw the prostitute, Thomas grabbed a burning branch and chased her out of his room. According to tradition, two angels came to him that night to strengthen him in his determination to remain celibate.

It is important to understand that the virtue of chastity is not identical to sexual abstinence or celibacy. Rather, everyone is called to be chaste. This virtue means integrating one's sexuality in a balanced and godly way with one's whole personality and vocation in life, whether single, married, or celibate.

CHILDREN
St. Nicholas of Myra
DECEMBER 6

*B*est known as the saint on whom the figure of Santa Claus is based, Nicholas was born early in the fourth century, most likely in Patara, Lycia, in Asia Minor, to wealthy parents. He was ordained a priest and named bishop of Myra. In time he gained a reputation for holiness, generosity, and miracles. During the persecution of Christians by the Roman emperor Diocletian, Nicholas was thrown in prison for his faith. Unaccountably released, he attended the Council of Nicaea, where he stood up and loudly denounced the Arian heresy. He died in Myra around the year 350.

Many entertaining—and sometimes inspirational—legends have developed around this saint. According to one story, when his rich parents died, he dedicated himself to the conversion of unbelievers and those who had abandoned the practice of the faith, and he gave all his money away to the poor. In another story, Nicholas appeared during a storm and calmed it, keeping a ship from sinking. And on another occasion, Nicholas appeared in a dream to the emperor Constantine to tell him that three Roman army officers who had been condemned to death at Constantinople were innocent. Constantine freed the officers the next morning.

Many stories recount Nicholas' generosity, which contributed to his identification as Santa Claus. In the most famous story, the father of three poor girls was on the verge of forcing his daughters into prostitution because he had no dowry for them. On three different nights, Nicholas surreptitiously tossed a bag of gold into the girls' house, and all three were able to marry.

Nicholas' popularity increased even more in the West when his relics were moved to Bari, Italy, in 1087. His shrine there became a major pilgrimage site in medieval Europe. Nicholas is the patron saint of children because of his particular generosity to young people. His feast day is celebrated in many countries by giving gifts to children.

29

CONVERTS
St. Margaret Clitherow
MARCH 26

Margaret Clitherow was born in 1556 in the English city of York, the daughter a successful candle maker. She married John Clitherow, a wealthy butcher, in 1571, and they had three children. A few years after her marriage, during the reign of Queen Elizabeth when it was a crime to practice Catholicism in England, Margaret converted. According to her confessor, she felt spiritually unsatisfied by the new Protestant practices, and she was also inspired by the many Catholics who were willing to suffer in defense of their faith. Her husband remained Protestant but supported his wife's decision.

Her husband was fined time and again because Margaret refused to attend Protestant church services. She arranged for a priest to say Mass in her home or in a rented house, and her home became one of the most prominent "safe houses" for priests being pursued by the secular authorities. She also organized a Catholic school for children. She was imprisoned once and then released.

In 1584 she was confined to her home for sending her oldest son to France to receive a Catholic education. Two years later in 1586, she was arrested, and the legal authorities discovered a missal and vessels used for saying Mass in a secret hiding place in her home. She was tried and found guilty of hiding priests, which was a capital offense. She was executed by being crushed to death with an eight-hundred-pound weight.

In 1970 Margaret Clitherow was canonized by Pope Paul VI, who called her the "Pearl of York," and was also included among the Forty Martyrs of England and Wales.

Those planning to convert to Catholicism today will probably not experience the persecution that Margaret suffered, but sometimes the path to conversion is a bumpy one. We can pray for the intercession of St. Margaret on their behalf, and we can also encourage those in the process of converting to pray to St. Margaret for her support and love.

COOKS

St. Lawrence

AUGUST 10

St. Lawrence is one of the earliest martyr-saints for which there is a solid historical basis, although we have few details about his life. We know for certain that he was a one of the seven deacons of Rome under Pope Sixtus II, who reigned from 257 to 258, and that he was martyred for his faith in 258.

The emperor at the time of Sixtus' brief reign, Valerian, persecuted Christians and quickly condemned the pope to death. As Pope Sixtus was being led away to his execution, he predicted that Lawrence would follow him three days later. According to the story, Lawrence rejoiced.

As a deacon, Lawrence was in charge of the Church's goods and almsgiving. The most famous story about Lawrence says that the Roman prefect ordered him to produce all the various gold and silver vessels in the sacred rites. Lawrence replied that he would need some time to gather all of the treasures of the Church, so the prefect gave him three days to do so. Lawrence gathered the poor and disadvantaged of Rome and brought them to the prefect, and told him that they were the Church's treasures. The prefect was so furious that he decided to prolong Lawrence's suffering by roasting him alive on a grill. Lawrence bore his torture silently, but in the midst of his agony, he told the executioner to turn him over since he was cooked enough on one side. This story seems to be the reason for St. Lawrence's identification as the patron saint of cooks.

As heroic as this story is, in all likelihood Lawrence was beheaded just as Sixtus was. Regardless of the means, Lawrence's death and inspiring example led many in Rome to become Christians, including several senators who witnessed Lawrence's torture and death and were converted on the spot. It also was the beginning of the end of paganism in Rome. Lawrence's martyrdom inspired tremendous devotion, not only in the city, but throughout the entire Church.

According to legend, Lawrence was buried by the senators who had converted. They carried his body to the Campus Vereanus on the Via Tiburtina. Later a basilica was constructed on this site in his honor. In the Church's liturgical calendar, August 10 is a special feast day in honor of St. Lawrence.

31

DANCERS
St. Vitus
JUNE 15

St. Vitus was a third-century Christian martyr from Sicily. The only son of a senator named Hylas, Vitus was converted to Christianity by his tutor, Modestus, and his tutor's wife, Crescentia. Vitus was baptized without the knowledge of his parents. Modestus and Crescentia accompanied Vitus on journeys throughout Sicily. His miracles and the resulting conversions became widely known to Valerian, the administrator of Sicily, who tried to stop him. According to legend, Vitus and his two companions fled in a boat to Rome that was guided by an angel. There he exorcised an evil spirit from the son of the emperor Diocletian.

When Vitus refused to sacrifice to the pagan gods, the healing of the emperor's son was attributed to sorcery. Vitus, Modestus, and Crescentia were tortured in various ways—including being placed into a pot of molten lead—but they were unharmed. They were tossed into the den of a hungry lion, but the beast merely licked Vitus' feet like a friendly house cat. We know nothing of how the three were ultimately martyred, only that they died for their Christian faith. One story says that they were placed on an instrument of torture called the iron horse, which stretched their bodies until all their limbs were dislocated. Though when they lived is uncertain, most stories place their martyrdom at the time of the emperor Diocletian, around the year 303.

Although these stories of how Vitus was martyred are legendary, age-old devotion to him and his companions is factual. There is an ancient church dedicated to St. Vitus on the Esquiline Hill in Rome. Vitus' relics were moved in 775 to the Church of Saint-Denis in Paris. A great devotion to Vitus developed in Germany when his relics were transferred to Corvey Abbey in Saxony in 836. Most of the medieval abbeys in England celebrated Vitus and Modestus without Crescentia, but others included her name.

In the late Middle Ages, people in Germany, Latvia, and other countries celebrated the feast of St. Vitus by dancing before his statue. The practice led to the naming of a neurological disorder called chorea, characterized by abnormal involuntary movements, as "St. Vitus' Dance." It also led to St. Vitus' patronage of dancers.

St. Vitus is included among the so-called "Fourteen Holy Helpers," who as a group are venerated widely in France and Germany. The relics of Vitus are said to possess many healing properties for those who pray before them, especially for those with epilepsy. Vitus is also the patron of those with epilepsy.

DEACONS
St. Stephen
DECEMBER 26

*E*verything we know about St. Stephen comes from the Acts of the Apostles—chapters six and seven, to be precise. Stephen was among the first group of deacons and belonged to a family of Hellenistic Jews, so he spoke Greek.

According to Acts, the Hellenistic Jews complained to the Hebrews that their widows were not receiving their fair share in the daily distribution of alms (6:1). As a way of resolving the problem, the apostles asked the Greek Jews to select seven men of good standing to be in charge of serving the needs of the poor. The first name listed is Stephen's. St. Luke, the author of Acts, says that Stephen was "full of grace and power" and "did great wonders and signs among the people" (6:8). Stephen was so zealous for his faith that he successfully debated with four different groups in the Greek-speaking synagogues. Then he was seized, dragged before the court of the Sanhedrin, and accused of blasphemy.

When the high priest asked Stephen if he had any response to his accusers, he gave a long speech tracing the sacred history of the Jews from Abraham to his own time. The men in the court were enraged and grabbed Stephen, took him outside the city, and stoned him to death. Stephen prayed aloud as he was being stoned, asking God to forgive his executioners.

Like Stephen, today's deacons continue to dedicate themselves to service, particularly within the local faith community. St. Stephen's active faith, even to the point of martyrdom, serves well as a model for deacons everywhere.

DENTISTS
St. Apollonia
FEBRUARY 9

The account of St. Apollonia comes from Dionysius, who was bishop of Alexandria from 247 to 265 and wrote about the martyrdom in a letter to the bishop of Antioch. According to his letter, a deaconess named Apollonia was seized by a crowd of men during an anti-Christian riot. They demanded that she renounce her Christian faith. When she refused to do so, all her teeth were broken—accounts vary as to whether they were broken by blows to her jaw or pulled out with pincers.

She was then taken to a fire and told that she would be burned alive unless she spoke blasphemy or prayed to a pagan god. As if wanting to consider her options, she begged for some additional time, and then jumped into the flames on her own. St. Augustine of Hippo later remarked that Apollonia must have acted under specific guidance from the Holy Spirit, because "when God gives a command and makes it clearly known, who would account obedience there to a crime or condemn such pious devotion and ready service?" (*The City of God*, 1:26).

Because one of her tortures was to have her teeth knocked or pulled out, St. Apollonia is the patron saint of dentists. Especially in the days before dental care, those with tooth pain called on this saint for relief, and she can still be called on today for anyone dealing with dental problems.

34

DESPERATE SITUATIONS
St. Jude
OCTOBER 28

St. Jude is called Thaddaeus in the Gospels of Matthew and Mark and Judas in the Gospel of Luke and the Book of Acts. He was a brother of the apostle James the Lesser and a relative of Jesus. Jude was the one who asked Jesus at the Last Supper why he would reveal himself to the apostles but not to the whole world (John 14:22).

Ancient writers tell us that Jude preached the gospel in Judea, Samaria, Idumaea, Syria, Mesopotamia, and Libya. According to the ancient historian Eusebius, he returned to Jerusalem in the year 62 and assisted at the election of his brother, Simeon, as bishop of Jerusalem. Legend claims that he visited Beirut and Edessa, and he may have been martyred in Persia along with Simon the Zealot. No doubt he died sometime in the late first century; according to Armenian tradition, he was martyred in the year 65. Sts. Simon and Jude share the feast day of October 28. Sometime after his death, his body was brought to Rome and is now in a crypt at St. Peter's Basilica.

St. Jude is invoked in desperate or hopeless situations, perhaps because the Letter of Jude in the New Testament encourages the faithful to persevere and protect the faith in an especially difficult situation, in which "certain intruders have stolen in among you" (verse 4).

Devotion to St. Jude in the United States became popular in 1929, when Fr. James Tort, a member of the Claretian Order, founded a shrine in the saint's honor in Chicago, Illinois. This shrine attracted people struggling with the poverty of the Great Depression of the 1930s. Even today, many people attend communal novenas to St. Jude. Noteworthy sites of devotion to St. Jude are the two parish churches of St. Francis of Assisi and St. Catherine of Siena in New York City. Of course, the original Shrine of St. Jude in Chicago continues to attract many people as well.

Probably the best-known story of St. Jude involves the late comedian and entertainer Danny Thomas. During the dark days of the Great Depression, praying for St. Jude's intercession, he promised God that if he helped him find his way in life, he would one day build a shrine to the saint. Soon after Thomas had his first success in show business. The now world-famous St. Jude Children's Research Hospital in Memphis, Tennessee, is the fulfillment of that promise.

35

Disabled People
St. Giles
September 1

*B*orn around the year 650, Giles was a citizen of Athens. However, he became the object of hero worship because of his miracles, so he left Athens to escape the adulation and went to southern France. There he lived as a hermit near the mouth of the Rhone River.

According to a legend about him, Giles was so impoverished that he survived off the milk of a deer. One day the deer took shelter with him to escape a royal hunting party. When one of the hunters shot an arrow at the deer, Giles was struck in the leg. The king sent doctors to care for the hermit's wound and often visited him. Some time later the king built a monastery and installed Giles as the abbot. He attracted many followers, who sought his wisdom and prayers.

St. Giles died in the early part of the eighth century. Because of his reputation for miracles and sanctity, a shrine around his tomb at the monastery Saint-Gilles-du-Gard became a major medieval pilgrimage site. In medieval art, St. Giles is often shown with a deer. Due to his damaged leg, Giles is the patron of persons with disabilities. He is also the patron of beggars, since begging was the only way for many disabled people to survive in those times.

36

Divorced People
St. Helena
August 18

Also known as Helen and sometimes Ellen, St. Helena was the mother of the first Christian Roman emperor, Constantine. She was born about the year 250 into a family of little or no social status in northwestern Asia Minor. Some sources say she was the daughter of an innkeeper. While working as a servant, Helena met and married the Roman general Constantius Chlorus, and in 285 they had a son, Constantine.

However, after twenty-two years of marriage, Constantius divorced Helena so that he could marry the daughter of the emperor and thus become emperor himself. After the death of Constantius in 306, Constantine succeeded his father and became emperor. Constantine held his mother in great esteem, granting her many honors, including the title Augusta, or empress. She had a great deal of influence in the imperial court.

About the year 312, when she was already past the age of sixty, Helena converted to Christianity. She adopted a simple lifestyle, gave generously to the poor and to parish churches, and visited prisoners. She also made a pilgrimage to the Holy Land, and there she built churches on the Mount of Olives and in Bethlehem. She also collected relics and gave generously to convents.

Helena is credited in ancient sources as well as in a sermon written by St. Ambrose (c. 338–397) with discovering Jesus' cross.

According to the story, in about 320 Helena led excavators to a place where three crosses were found buried. Having no way to discover which one was Jesus' cross, the bishop of Jerusalem sent a woman who was dying to the spot. She was told to touch the three crosses, and when she touched the third cross, she was instantly healed, thus revealing the cross upon which Jesus was crucified.

Helena died in Nicomedia (modern Turkey) in 330. Later her body was taken to Rome, where it was placed in a tomb connected to the Church of Sts. Peter and Marcellinus. Ever since the ninth century, however, the monastery of Hautvillers, close to Reims, France, has insisted that her body is there.

Divorce is an emotionally wrenching experience, so Catholics can turn to this saint for her intercession, whether they are going through a divorce themselves or are close to someone who is. Catholics who are divorced can continue to receive the sacraments as long as they do not remarry—and in some cases, they can seek to have their marriages annulled. St. Helena shows us that even something as tragic as a failed marriage does not prevent us from bearing much fruit for the Lord.

Drug Addicts
St. Maximilian Kolbe
August 14

*B*orn on January 7, 1894, near Lodz, Poland, Raymond Kolbe had a reputation for being a mischievous child. However, one day in 1906 when he was twelve years old, he had a vision of the Blessed Virgin Mary that changed his life.

"I asked the Mother of God what was to become of me," Kolbe wrote. "Then she came to me holding two crowns, one white, the other red. She asked if I was willing to accept either of these crowns. The white one meant that I should persevere in purity, and the red that I should become a martyr. I said that I would accept them both."

Raymond entered the Conventual Franciscans and took the name Maximilian. To promote devotion to the Blessed Virgin, he founded an organization called the Militia of Mary Immaculate in Rome. He was ordained a priest in Rome in 1918. About this time he contracted tuberculosis, so he returned to Poland to recuperate. There he started a monthly magazine called *Militia of the Immaculate Mary*.

In 1827 he founded a Franciscan commune called Niepokalanów (City of the Immaculate Conception) twenty-five miles from Warsaw, which became home to about eight hundred Conventual Franciscan men. He traveled to and started similar communes in Japan and India. In 1936 he was named superior of the Polish Niepokalanów.

In 1941, following the Nazi invasion of Poland, Fr. Kolbe was arrested by the Gestapo and imprisoned in the infamous death camp Auschwitz. One day ten men were arbitrarily chosen by the Nazi commandant to be executed because one prisoner had escaped. Fr. Kolbe volunteered to take the place of a married man with a family and was held in a cell and left to starve to death. Over the next three weeks, Kolbe encouraged the other men, prayed with them, and sang hymns. On August 14, 1941, he was the only man who had not died, so he was killed with an injection of carbolic acid. He was beatified by Pope Paul VI in 1971 and canonized by Pope John Paul II on October 10, 1982.

Fr. Kolbe was named the patron of drug addicts because he died for Christ by means of a hypodermic needle. However, in submitting to this kind of death, St. Maximilian Kolbe was choosing life, not death. Thus he intercedes for those who want to leave needles of death behind.

38

Emigrants and Immigrants
St. Frances Xavier Cabrini
December 22

The first American citizen to be canonized, Frances Xavier Cabrini was born in Italy on July 15, 1850. She was the youngest of thirteen children of parents who were farmers. When she was thirteen, Frances was sent to Arluno to study under the Daughters of the Sacred Heart. In 1868, when she was eighteen, she received a teaching certificate. A few years later when she applied to enter the Daughters of the Sacred Heart, she was refused because of her poor health. She was turned down by another community as well.

So Frances helped on the family farm and supported her parents until they died. She then taught at a private school. In 1871, at the request of the pastor of her parish, she became a teacher in a school in a village near her home. In 1877 she took private religious vows and added Xavier to her name in honor of the famous Jesuit missionary priest, St. Francis Xavier. She was given charge of an orphanage in Codogno, where she taught.

In 1880, when the orphanage was closed, Frances and six other women who took religious vows with her founded the Institute of the Missionary Sisters of the Sacred Heart of Jesus (MSC). On

November 14 of that year, Mother Cabrini wrote the rule and constitution of the new religious order, and she served as its superior general until her death.

In her community's first five years, Mother Cabrini founded seven homes and a free school and nursery. The success of Mother Cabrini's charitable works brought her and her community to the attention of the bishop of Piacenza and then of Pope Leo XIII. Mother Cabrini's dream had been to be a missionary in China, but in 1889 the pope sent her to New York City to minister to poor Italian immigrants.

Once there, she gained the permission of Archbishop Michael Corrigan to found an orphanage. (Today that facility in New York is known as St. Cabrini Home and cares for adolescents with emotional problems.) The bishop begged her to also start hospitals for the immigrants, but Mother Cabrini was reluctant until she had a dream in which she saw the Blessed Virgin Mary tending to a hospital patient. When she asked Mary what she was doing, Mary responded, "I am doing the work you refuse to do."

In all, Mother Cabrini founded sixty-seven schools, orphanages, and hospitals throughout the country and in South America and Europe. She became an American citizen in 1909. She died on December 22, 1917, in Chicago of complications from malaria, which she had contracted on a trip to South America.

In an era when immigration is a controversial issue, we may want to cultivate a devotion to St. Frances Xavier Cabrini as we intercede for the plight of immigrants in our own country and in others. Mother Cabrini is a reminder of the great potential of those who come across our borders seeking a new home.

ENGAGED COUPLES
St. Agnes
JANUARY 21

*A*s with many saints from the early centuries of the Church, we don't know when St. Agnes was born, but we have a general idea of when she died—about the year 305. Agnes was one of the best known of the early martyrs and is among those killed for their faith during the Roman persecution of Christians. She undoubtedly died at a very young age, probably twelve or thirteen, during the persecution carried out by the emperor Diocletian.

Agnes was beautiful and came from a wealthy Roman Christian family. Early in her life, she consecrated herself to God as a virgin. Nevertheless, she had suitors, and it was one of them who, frustrated by Agnes' refusal, exposed her as a Christian to the governor. When Agnes was arrested, despite her youth she refused to be intimidated when she was shown the instruments of torture. Ordered to offer sacrifice to idols, Agnes instead knelt down and made the sign of the cross. Furious, the governor sent Agnes to a house of prostitution, where she still managed to retain her virginity by her displays of courage and faith. According to one story, a young man who tried to take Agnes by force was struck dead by lightning. The young man's friends carried his body to Agnes, who prayed for him, and he was restored to life.

When Agnes was again taken before the governor, he showed great frustration at being opposed by a young girl and condemned her to death. The executioner had been ordered to try to change Agnes' mind, but nothing he could do or say turned her from her faith. Agnes said a short prayer, then willingly placed her head on the chopping block. With one stroke of his sword, the executioner beheaded Agnes.

While the details of this story are far from trustworthy, there is no doubt that Agnes died a martyr for her faith. She was buried on the Via Nomentana, just outside Rome, and fifty years later the Christian emperor Constantine erected a basilica there in her honor.

Agnes is often represented in art with a lamb because her name is similar to *agnus*, the Latin word for "lamb." Each year on the feast of St. Agnes, two lambs are brought to her basilica and blessed, and then are raised to produce the wool used to make the palliums or stoles given to archbishops.

We may wonder why St. Agnes is the patron saint of engaged couples, since she herself didn't want to marry. Aside from the fact that there are no canonized engaged persons, we do well simply to trust the sacred tradition that gives us St. Agnes in this role. She no doubt relishes the role herself.

ENGINEERS
St. Ferdinand III of Castile
MAY 30

Ferdinand III was a model ruler for his times. He was a faith-filled, practical, and effective administrator, founding hospitals, monasteries, and churches. He established a lasting peace in both of his kingdoms, Castile and León. His contemporaries described him as being strict in his administration of justice but always ready to forgive personal injuries and offenses. He also reclaimed much of southern Spain from the Moors.

Born about the year 1199, Ferdinand became king at the age of eighteen when his mother, the daughter of King Alfonso III of Castile in Spain, gave up her claim to the throne. When his father, King Alfonso IX of León, died in 1230, Ferdinand also became king of León—despite objections from his two half sisters.

Two years into his reign, in 1219, Ferdinand married the daughter of King Philip of Swabia, Germany, whose name was Beatrice. Together they had seven sons and three daughters. For some twenty-seven years, he fought the Moors who controlled much of southern Spain. He eventually drove them out of Ubeda, Cordova, Murcia, Jaen, Cadiz, and in 1249, from Seville itself. At one battle he personally led, St. James was seen riding a white horse and leading the Spanish army against the enemy.

Ferdinand's chancellor and main adviser for many years was an archbishop named Rodrigo Ximenes, who ably assisted him in founding the great University of Salamanca in 1243, rebuilding the cathedral in Burgos, and converting a mosque in Seville into a church. Perhaps because of these accomplishments, which often required engineering know-how, he is the patron of engineers.

Ferdinand died on May 30, 1252, and was buried in the cathedral in Seville. A Third Order Franciscan, he was buried wearing the religious habit of a Franciscan friar. He was canonized a saint in 1671 by Pope Clement X.

41

EXPECTANT MOTHERS
St. Gerard Majella
OCTOBER 16

One may understandably question why a man—and a celibate lay brother in a religious order at that—would be the patron saint of expectant mothers. But St. Gerard has a history of hearing the prayers of expectant mothers and of women who are trying to conceive.

Gerard was born in 1726 in Muro, a small town in southern Italy. As a young child, he was often frail and sick. When Gerard was five years old, he regularly visited a chapel near his home. To his parents' surprise, he often returned home with a loaf of bread. When asked where the bread came from, he replied that a little boy gave it to him. One day his older sister, Elizabeth, followed Gerard to the chapel. She watched him as he knelt to pray before a statue of the Blessed Mother holding the child Jesus. Soon Jesus left his mother's arms and joined Gerard in play. Later the child gave Gerard a loaf of bread and returned to his mother.

Gerard, whose father was a tailor, worked as a tailor's apprentice. When he tried to join the Capuchins, he was refused for being too young. Instead, he became a servant in the household of the bishop of Lacedonga. When the bishop died in 1745, Gerard returned home and opened a tailor shop. When he was twenty-three years old, he joined the Redemptorists and became a lay brother. The priest before whom he made his vows was the founder of the order, St. Alphonsus Liguori.

Gerard served as sacristan, gardener, porter, infirmarian, and tailor. He became known for his deep spirituality, profound wisdom, and his gift of reading consciences. Although not a priest, he was permitted to counsel communities of women religious. He also regularly experienced extraordinary spiritual phenomena such as levitation and bilocation. His compassionate charity, obedience, and selfless service made him an ideal model for lay brothers. Because he attracted huge numbers of people who wanted him to pray for them, he was moved from community to community, but the crowds inevitably followed. Gerard contracted tuberculosis and died in 1755 at the age of twenty-nine.

Even before he was canonized in 1904, pregnant women and those in labor began praying for the intercession of St. Gerard Majella. Indeed, he is known as a "thaumaturge" or wonder-worker—a saint whose intercession results in miracles not just occasionally but regularly. It is said that God raises up such a saint only once every century.

St. Gerard is as popular today as he has been over the centuries. In fact, several Web sites are dedicated to St. Gerard and his intercession for expectant mothers and those who desire to have children. According to one site, a woman was told she would never have another child after her first son was born. She prayed for St. Gerard's intercession and subsequently gave birth to fifteen children!

FARMERS
St. Isidore
MAY 15

St. Isidore lived simply and virtuously, committed to family, love for the land, service to the poor, and a deep faith in God. His life is a testament to the inherent dignity of manual labor or of any work that is done with integrity and for the glory of God.

Isidore was born in Madrid in 1070 to devout parents who were so poor that they were unable to care for the boy. They sent him to work for a wealthy landowner near Madrid, and Isidore worked for this man for the rest of his life.

He married Maria Torribia, a woman who would later be declared a saint under the name St. Maria de la Cabeza. The couple had one son who died in childhood. Grief stricken, they concluded that his death was a sign from God to live a life of celibacy. (Of course, neither Church teachings nor contemporary spiritual theology would support such a conclusion today.)

Because Isidore attended Mass at his parish church every morning, he was often late for work. According to legend, on such occasions his plowing of the fields was done by angels, who accomplished three times as much work as Isidore would have. The future saint's co-workers and his employer witnessed these miraculous events, and as a result Isidore was held in high esteem.

Not only did Isidore had a deep love for the poor, his affection for animals rivaled that of St. Francis of Assisi. A well-known miracle of the multiplication of food occurred when Isidore fed grain to a flock of starving birds and still had the same amount of grain leftover. A similar miracle happened when Isidore shared his meal with a large crowd of beggars.

Isidore died on May 15, 1120, when he was sixty years old. He was canonized in 1622 along with four other saints: St. Ignatius of Loyola, St. Teresa of Ávila, St. Francis Xavier, and St. Philip Neri. The body of St. Isidore is incorrupt.

In addition to being the patron saint of farmers, St. Isidore is the patron of the United States National Rural Life Conference. His wife, Maria, is the patron saint of farm wives. Her feast day is September 14.

FATHERS
St. Joseph
MARCH 19

St. Joseph is the husband of the Blessed Virgin Mary and the foster father of Jesus. He makes his main appearances in the infancy narratives of Matthew (1–2) and Luke (1–2), where we learn that he was descended from David. Luke says that Joseph was from Bethlehem but lived in Nazareth with Mary, going back to Bethlehem only to register for a census (2:1). Matthew seems to indicate that the couple lived in Bethlehem, moving later to Nazareth after the flight to Egypt (2:22-23). Matthew also says that Joseph was a carpenter (13:55) while the Gospel of Mark clearly implies that Joseph trained Jesus as a carpenter (6:3).

Betrothed to Joseph, Mary was already pregnant when Joseph took her into his home to live with him. According to Deuteronomy 22:20-21, a betrothed woman who was unfaithful was to be stoned to death. Initially, because he was a good man, Joseph decided to quietly divorce Mary. However, an angel told Joseph in a dream to take Mary into his home because her child was conceived through divine means. In a second dream, after the birth of Jesus, the angel told Joseph to take Mary and the child to Egypt to escape the mass murder of newborn boys.

The last mention of Joseph is in Luke's narrative concerning the pilgrimage to Jerusalem when Jesus was twelve years old (2:42-52). Because he is not mentioned again, the conclusion traditionally drawn is that Joseph must have died prior to the beginning of Jesus' public ministry.

The veneration of Joseph is said to have begun in the East when the Coptic Christian Church observed a feast in honor of St. Joseph in the seventh century. The earliest indication of a similar veneration in the West is in Irish documents from the ninth century. From the 1300s on, various notable saints encouraged devotion to St. Joseph. In 1870, at the conclusion of the First Vatican Council, Pope Pius IX declared Joseph to be the patron of the universal Church. Joseph is also the patron saint of a happy death, workers, and various countries. Many religious congregations, Church-related institutions, and churches are named for St. Joseph. In 1962 Pope John XXIII added the name of St. Joseph to the Canon of the Mass, now called the First Eucharistic Prayer.

In these days, when so many fathers are absent from their children, it is especially important for families to ask for Joseph's intercession and help. He is the model father and protector. The fact that God chose him for the important role of caring for and raising Jesus shows us just how crucial fathers are in the life of the family.

FIREFIGHTERS
St. Florian
MAY 4

*A*n officer in the Roman army, Florian held an important administrative position in Noricum (which is now a part of Austria). He was killed in the year 304 for refusing direct orders to execute Christians during the persecution carried out by the emperor Diocletian. There is probably historical basis to the story that Florian willingly surrendered himself to soldiers who had been sent to take him prisoner. He gladly proclaimed his Christian faith and was scourged twice, and the flesh was stripped from half his body. He was thrown into the Enns River with a large stone tied around his neck.

An eagle was said to have watched over Florian's body until it was recovered by a local Christian woman and buried. Later his body was exhumed and taken to an Augustinian abbey near Linz. Some historians believe that St. Florian's body was subsequently taken to Rome and that Pope Lucius III in 1138 sent some of the saint's relics to King Casimir of Poland and some to the bishop of Krakow. Ever since, there has been a great deal of popular devotion to St. Florian in parts of central Europe. One tradition, which is both ancient and reliable, identifies the spot of his martyrdom as a location not far from where the Enns River joins the Danube.

Numerous healing miracles have been attributed to St. Florian's intercession, and he is turned to by those in danger from fire or water. According to legend, Florian saved an entire village from fire by dousing it with a single bucket of water. Medals of St. Florian are sometimes available from Catholic gift shops. No doubt there are many firefighters who would appreciate having such a medal.

45

Forest Workers
St. John Gualbert
July 12

A member of a noble family, John Gualbert was born in Florence, Italy, in the year 999. As a young adult, he became a soldier and embraced a dissolute life. Riding into Florence with his fellow soldiers one Good Friday, John encountered the man who had murdered his brother, Hugh.

He would have killed the man, according to the custom of vengeance of those times, but his brother's murderer fell on his knees with his arms outstretched in the form of a cross and begged John, for the sake of the Lord Jesus, to spare his life. John replied that he could not refuse what was asked in the name of Christ. Then he told his adversary that he would give him not only his life but his friendship. The two men then embraced and went their separate ways.

A humbled and changed man, John went to a nearby church. While he prayed sincerely for forgiveness, the figure of the crucified Lord before which he was kneeling bowed his head toward him. John entered the Order of St. Benedict and devoted himself to prayer and the monastic life. His virtue and simplicity were so admired by his fellow monks that when the abbot of the monastery died, John was unanimously chosen to become the new abbot. John, however, refused to accept that honor. Instead, he retired to Vallombrosa, where a new religious order, the Vallombrosans, was started that also followed the Rule of St. Benedict. It was from this place, not far from Florence, that the new order spread over all of Italy. John never became a priest, and his order lived in poverty and cared for the sick in the monastery hospice.

John's patronage of forest workers seems to come from the fact that the forested land upon which he built his monastery was given to him by the abbess of a convent nearby (the name Vallombrosa means "Shady Valley").

Once during a famine, it was said that John went to the nearly empty storeroom and prayed, and the provisions multiplied so that he was able to distribute food to the poor. Another time some men who opposed John plundered one of his order's monasteries and beat the monks severely. John rejoiced, telling them, "Now you are true monks. How I envy your lot!"

St. John Gualbert fought with all his strength against simony, the selling of pardons and Church offices. After a life of great holiness, he died on July 12, 1073. According to legend, angels sang near his bed.

FRIENDSHIP
St. John the Evangelist
DECEMBER 27

St. John, an apostle and the author of the gospel that bears his name, was a special friend of Jesus—"the one whom Jesus loved" (John 13:23)—so it is appropriate that he is the patron of friendship.

From the gospels we know that John was born in Galilee and was the son of Zebedee and the younger brother of James. He was a fisherman when he and James were called by Jesus to follow him (Matthew 4:21-22; Mark 1:19-20). Evidently he was the youngest of the twelve apostles, and he and his brother James were nicknamed "the Sons of Thunder" by Jesus, probably because they were quick to anger (Mark 3:17).

John was part of the inner circle of disciples, along with James and Peter, who were privileged to see such events as Jesus' transfiguration (Matthew 17:1), the healing of Peter's mother-in-law (Mark 1:29-31), the raising of Jairus' daughter from the dead (Mark 5:35-42), and Jesus' agony in the Garden of Gethsemane (Matthew 36-36; Mark 14:32-36). John and Peter were sent to make preparations for the Passover (Luke 22:8), and they were the first apostles to arrive at the empty tomb of Jesus (John 20:2-10).

John was the only apostle who remained at the foot of the cross when Jesus was crucified, and from the cross, Jesus gave his mother into the care of John (John 19:26-27). John was imprisoned with Peter and appeared with Peter to address the Sanhedrin (Acts 4:10-21), and he was Peter's companion when they went to Samaria to pray with a group of converts to receive the Holy Spirit (Acts 8:14). John also attended the Council of Jerusalem in the year 49.

According to oral tradition, soon after this council, John went to Asia Minor. In his Letter to the Galatians, St. Paul acknowledged John, Peter, and James as "pillars" of the church in Jerusalem (2:9).

According to tradition, John went to Rome during the reign of the emperor Domitian but miraculously escaped martyrdom. He was exiled to the island of Patmos. John is sometimes identified as the same John who authored the Book of Revelation, but there is no scholarly consensus on this point. When the emperor Domitian died in 96, John is said to have returned to Ephesus and written his gospel. More likely, the Gospel of John was redacted and edited by other hands using materials that may have come from him and his community.

Friendship is important in all our lives, especially in the lives of Christians, who need the support and love of their brothers and sisters on their journey of faith. If you are looking for Christian friends or need help with a friendship, ask for the intercession of St. John, who enjoyed such a deep friendship with Jesus.

FUNERAL DIRECTORS
St. Joseph of Arimathea
MARCH 17

Poor St. Joseph of Arimathea has the unfortunate distinction of having the same feast day as St. Patrick. Guess which one gets the most attention!

We know from all four gospels that Joseph was a secret follower of Jesus. Joseph was present at the crucifixion of Jesus, and after his death, Joseph asked Pontius Pilate if he could have Jesus' body for burial. Joseph wrapped Jesus' body in linen with spices and placed it in a tomb that he owned, which was hollowed out of rock in the side of a hill (John 19:38-40; Mark 15:42-26).

That's the only historical information we have of Joseph. As so often happens with saints, legends tend to fill in the gaps. According to a medieval legend, Joseph caught some of Jesus' blood in a cup as he hung upon the cross. As a faithful disciple of the apostle Philip, Joseph took this blood to Gaul, where together they preached the gospel. Later he was sent to England as the head of twelve missionaries. Directed by the archangel Gabriel to an island, Joseph and his twelve companions built a church there in honor of Mary. The church was made of wattles, a construction of poles intertwined with twigs, reeds, or branches. According to the legend, this church eventually became Glastonbury Abbey. Joseph is also supposed to have come into possession of the chalice used by Jesus at the Last Supper—the Holy Grail, about which there is no lack of legends.

Burying the dead a corporal act of mercy. Joseph will be honored for all time for his care of Jesus' body after the crucifixion. There was a time, of course, when care of the dead and preparation of bodies for burial were family concerns. Today funeral directors assist families with this important act of charity.

GARDENERS
St. Adelard
JANUARY 2

*A*delard was the first cousin of Charlemagne. In 773, when he was about twenty years old, he entered a French monastery in Corbie, Picardy. His first assignment was to be a gardener, but soon after he was elected abbot. He is often represented as an abbot digging a garden, with a crown nearby.

Charlemagne frequently required Adelard to be present in his court as an adviser, and he soon became the king's chief counselor. Eventually Charlemagne appointed Adelard chief minister of his son, Pepin, king of Italy. After Pepin's death in 810, Adelard became tutor to Pepin's son, Bernard.

When Charlemagne died in 814, Adelard was accused of treason and banished to a monastery on the little island of Héri off the coast of Aquitaine. Adelard was perfectly happy with this turn of events since he loved monastic life. After five years, however, it came to light that Adelard was innocent of the charge against him, and the emperor Bernard called him back to the royal court in 821. After a short period of time, Adelard insisted on returning to his monastery in Picardy, and there he was happy to be responsible for the most humble tasks. Adelard made a special effort to inquire about the welfare of each and every monk, and he welcomed advice from any of his brothers in the monastery.

He was loved by all his fellow monks as well as the neighbors who lived near the monastery.

Adelard zealously promoted literature in his monastery. He instructed the people who lived near the monastery, not only in Latin, but also in the Teutonic and French languages. Fragments of some of Adelard's writings survive to this day.

St. Adelard had just returned from a visit to Germany three days before Christmas when he became ill. He died on January 2, 827, at the age of seventy-three. Several miracles were attributed to Adelard's intercession, and in 1040 he was declared a saint. A detailed account exists of the canonization ceremony, written by an author in gratitude for having been cured of head pains after praying for Adelard's intercession.

Even though Adelard was a nobleman and a scholar, he cultivated the humility to work at gardening as well. He understood that gardening gives glory to the Creator, who is also our loving Father.

Grandmothers
St. Anne
July 26

The *Infancy Gospel of James* was a widely circulated apocryphal gospel, probably written around the year 150. It tells the story of Mary's birth and identifies her parents as Anne and Joachim. Though it is not considered to have historical validity and was never accepted in the canon of books that make up the Bible, the narrative does attest to the early veneration of Mary.

According to this gospel, Anne and Joachim were a rich and childless couple living in Nazareth. One day Joachim went to the Temple to offer sacrifice but was told he could not do so because he was childless and therefore unworthy. He went into the mountains in solitude to pray. Anne learned why he had not returned and cried out to the Lord for a child, promising to dedicate this child in service to the Lord. An angel appeared to her and said, "The Lord has looked upon your tears; you shall conceive and give birth, and the fruit of your womb shall be blessed by all the world." The angel made the same promise to Joachim, and he returned. Then Anne gave birth to a daughter, whom she named Miriam or Mary. The story resembles the biblical account of Hannah and her conception of Samuel.

Veneration of St. Anne became very popular in the West after the publication of *The Golden Legend*, a collection of stories about the saints written by Jacopo de Voragine. Even Anne's supposed relics were venerated in various places in Europe.

We don't have reliable information about the grandmother of Jesus, and even her name is unknown. However, Mary did have a mother, and Jesus did have a grandmother. Like any grandmother, this woman must surely have delighted in her special grandson. We may cultivate devotion to St. Anne with this prayer:

Families that are truly Christian love the family of Nazareth, but they also honor the parents of Mary, especially St. Anne who bore and gave birth to her. How glorious to give birth to one who would be the Mother of God! May we who have devotion to you, St. Anne, obtain even more devotion to Mary and the greatest devotion to Christ, your grandson. Amen.

50

Headache Sufferers
St. Teresa of Ávila
October 15

St. Teresa of Ávila was a Carmelite mystic and reformer whose writings on prayer have guided countless Christians over the past five hundred years. Teresa had many gifts; she was beautiful, intelligent, and also very practical. All her life, in an era when men held the power in both the world and the Church, she stood up for her beliefs and prevailed.

Teresa was born on March 28, 1515, in Ávila in the Castile region of Spain. Educated by Augustinian nuns, she left the convent school in 1532 because of ill health. She was attracted to the religious life, and in 1536 she joined the Carmelite Order in Ávila even though her father opposed it. She left in 1538 due to illness but returned several years later. She suffered from what modern scholars believe were migraine headaches all her adult life, as well as other health problems.

Teresa lived the ordinary life of a nun and tried to progress in prayer but was distracted by the casual environment of the convent. Finally one day in 1555, she knelt before a statute of the wounded Christ. Her heart broke as she thanked him for his wounds. From then on she experienced great visions and raptures. She considered these experiences favors from God for which she felt radically unworthy.

In 1561, in the face of bitter opposition from within her own order, she decided to break away from her convent and start another one with a stricter observance of the Carmelite rule. In 1562 she founded St. Joseph's Convent in Ávila. In 1567 Teresa received permission to establish other strict-observance convents, and in the years that followed, she founded sixteen such communities. While establishing her second convent at Medino del Campo, she met a young Carmelite friar, John of the Cross. In 1568, together with St. John, she founded her first reformed Carmelite monastery for men.

Teresa's writings on prayer and contemplation are timeless classics in which she drew from her own experience. Among these works is her autobiography, *The Book of Her Life*, as well as *The Way of Perfection* and *Interior Castle*. She died at Alba de Tormes, Spain, on October 14, 1582, and was canonized in 1622 by Pope Gregory XV. She was declared a doctor of the Church—the first woman to be thus honored—in 1970 by Pope Paul VI.

Many people today suffer from recurrent migraine headaches. If you know of someone who does, suggest that they ask for Teresa's intercession to be healed. Beyond headaches, however, Teresa is the saint we can turn to when we want to deepen our prayer life. She is a master teacher and can show us how to live in closer union with Jesus.

51

Holy Souls in Purgatory
St. Nicholas of Tolentino
September 10

Nicholas of Tolentino was born in 1245 in the village of Sant' Angelo in Ancona, Italy. His middle-aged parents had been childless and had made a pilgrimage to the shrine of St. Nicholas at Bari, where his mother begged God for a son who would serve Christ. So when Nicholas was born, he received the name of his patron.

As a boy Nicholas would often go to a small cave near Sant' Angelo to pray, imitating the hermits who lived among the Apennine Mountains. Today pilgrims go to this cave to pray for his intercession.

At the age of eighteen, Nicholas entered the Augustinian Order. He took his final vows in 1263 and was ordained a priest about 1270. After serving as master of novices, he was sent to Tolentino, where he worked as a peacemaker in a city torn by civil strife. He gained a reputation for his preaching and for his gifts as a confessor who converted hard-hearted sinners and cared for the poor, the sick, and criminals. He often fasted and spent long hours in prayer. Among his many miracles, he was reported to have resurrected over one hundred children from the dead, including several who had drowned.

After he had a vision in which Mary gave him a small piece of bread dipped in water to heal him of an illness, Nicholas was especially known for healing people with small pieces of bread. "St. Nicholas Bread" is still distributed on his feast day and at his shrine in Tolentino.

Nicholas had a special love for the souls in purgatory and prayed diligently for them. According to one story, he heard the voice of a recently deceased friar one night while he was asleep. The friar asked him to pray for him and to offer a Mass for him. He did so, and seven days later, the friar again spoke to him, thanking him and telling him that many souls were now with God because of his prayers. As patron of the holy souls in purgatory, Nicholas reminds us to seek his intercession when we are praying for our own loved ones who have died.

After laboring for thirty years and after a long illness, Nicholas died at Tolentino on September 10, 1305. Many miracles were attributed to his intercession. He was canonized in 1446.

52

THE HOMELESS
St. Benedict Joseph Labré
APRIL 16

Benedict Joseph Labré was born in Amettes, France, on March 25, 1748, the oldest of fifteen children of a shopkeeper. His uncle was the parish priest in the village of Erin. As a boy under his direction, Benedict received an elementary education. He tried with no success to join several monastic orders, including the Trappists and the Carthusians. Finally in 1770, at the age of twenty-two, he decided to become a lifelong pilgrim in imitation of Christ, who had "nowhere to lay his head" (Matthew 8:20).

In the course of his life as a pilgrim, Benedict Joseph Labré visited many of the major shrines and pilgrimage sites in Western Europe. His only possessions, besides the one set of clothes he wore, were two rosaries and three books: a New Testament, a Breviary, and a copy of *The Imitation of Christ*. In 1774 he took up residence permanently in Rome, where he spent his last years. He often slept in the Colosseum and became known as "the beggar of Rome" for his poverty and holiness.

Benedict spent his days in churches, especially those where the Forty Hours devotion happened to be in progress. His favorite church was Santa Maria dei Monti, where he had a special devotion to frescoes of the Madonna and Child and of Sts. Stephen, Lawrence, Augustine, and Francis of Assisi.

Toward the end of his life, he grew very ill and sometimes took shelter in a hospice for poor men. As Holy Week of 1783 approached, he was near death. On that Wednesday he collapsed just outside Santa Maria dei Monti after attending Mass. A local butcher picked him up off the street and carried him to his own nearby home. That evening, on April 16, 1783, he died. He was thirty-five years old. So great was the crowd thronging his funeral that troops had to be called to maintain public order.

A few months after the saint's death, some 130 miracles were attributed to Benedict's intercession. That year Fr. G. L. Marconi, the priest who had been Benedict's confessor, wrote and published a biography about him. St. Benedict Joseph Labré was canonized by Pope Leo XIII on December 8, 1881.

Part of the butcher's house where Benedict died was converted into a chapel with an altar and two cupboards containing the few possessions he left behind. A life-sized recumbent statue of the saint was installed in the very place where he died, and over the statue hangs a painting of the Blessed Virgin Mary. Benedict was buried beneath an altar in a chapel inside Santa Maria dei Monti, where there is another life-sized marble statue of him. The death mask that was made before his burial still exists.

This saint's life is a reminder of the inherent dignity of every human being, even those without a permanent home. If you are involved in helping the homeless—whether distributing food or clothing or just saying hello and offering a friendly smile—you can remember to pray for St. Benedict's intercession. He certainly has a special love for those who have nowhere to lay their heads.

53

HUMAN RIGHTS
Blessed Jerzy Popieluszko
OCTOBER 19

One of the modern martyrs of the faith, Fr. Jerzy Popieluszko was described by those who knew him as a simple person who was even shy at times. However, he was not shy about speaking out for basic human rights, which Christians believe are based on the dignity they derive from being made in God's image. During the 1980s, Fr. Popieluszko defended the rights of the people who were struggling against the Communist regime, which had ruled Poland since the end of World War II.

Born into a poor rural family in northeastern Poland, Jerzy entered Warsaw's Catholic seminary in 1965. He was ordained a priest in 1972 by another champion of the Polish people, Cardinal Stefan Wyszynski. Unfortunately, while still a seminarian, the young priest's health suffered from two years of military service, and health problems plagued him for the remainder of his life.

Following earlier pastoral assignments, in 1980 Fr. Popieluszko was sent to St. Stanislaw Kostka Church in Warsaw. From there he served as chaplain at the nearby Huta Warszawa steelworks during the August 1980 strikes, which led to the formation of the Solidarity labor union. In February of 1982, Solidarity was declared illegal by martial law. Soon after, Fr. Popieluszko presided at the first of numerous "Masses for the Homeland," a practice soon copied by other priests throughout Poland. Fr.

Popieluszko preached many sermons in support of basic human rights, such as freedom of speech and the right to organize in support of just labor practices. His sermons gave people hope in the midst of despair, and he became the spiritual director for the Solidarity movement.

Fr. Popieluszko was taken into custody and interrogated by government agents on several occasions. In July 1984 he was formally charged with "abusing the functions of a priest" and "anti-state propaganda." A month later the charges were suspended. On October 19, 1984, the priest was kidnapped as he returned to his parish in Warsaw from an evening Mass in a nearby city. While captive, he was brutally beaten. Eleven days later his bound and gagged body was recovered from a reservoir. He was thirty-seven years old.

Some four hundred thousand people attended the priest's funeral, and as of 2010, eighteen million people have visited his grave at the parish church where he served. The Archdiocese of Warsaw initiated a canonization process for Fr. Popieluszko in 2001, and he was beatified in Warsaw on June 6, 2010. His mother, Marianna, who was present at the beatification ceremony, said she has forgiven her son's murderers and prays for their conversion.

INFERTILITY
St. Rita of Cascia
MAY 22

Rita of Cascia was a wife and mother, then a widow, and finally a member of a religious community. She was born at Roccaporena near Spoleto in central Italy to middle-aged parents. Rita wanted to enter a convent, but at the age of twelve, she was pressured into marrying an unloving, cruel man. Married for eighteen years, Rita had two sons. Her husband was killed in a brawl between two warring factions in the city. Her sons swore revenge on their father's murderer, but then they died of natural causes.

Rita tried three times to join the Augustinian nuns in Cascia, but she was rejected each time because the nuns feared dissension in their community because of her family's violent past. Finally Rita was able to get the warring parties to sign a peace agreement. In 1413, at the age of thirty-six, she was accepted into the community.

Over time Rita became known for her holiness, her austerity and penances, and her charity to others. By her prayers she brought back to the Church many who had abandoned their faith. In 1441, when Rita developed wounds on her forehead, people soon connected them with the wounds from Christ's crown of thorns. She meditated frequently on Christ's passion. She exercised great kindness and concern for sick members of her community and gave spiritual counsel to laypeople who came to her monastery to consult with her.

Like St. Jude, St. Rita has acquired the reputation as a saint of impossible causes—in particular with regard to infertility. Certainly in her life she overcame many impossible situations, but a famous story about one particular situation also supports this link. While bedridden at the end of her life, her cousin visited her and asked if she wanted anything from her former home. She asked for a rose. Though it was the middle of January, her cousin found a single rose blooming in her garden. For this reason, Rita is often depicted with a rose.

Several miracles were attributed to Rita after her death on May 22, 1457. Rita was beatified in 1626 but was not canonized until 1900. Many pilgrims visit her tomb in Umbria each year.

LAWYERS
St. Thomas More
JUNE 22

St. Thomas More was a lawyer, a statesman, and one of the leading intellectuals of his time. He is also a saint and a martyr: He was beheaded for treason for refusing to take an oath accepting King Henry VIII's claim as supreme head of the English Church.

Thomas More was born in London on February 6, 1478, the son of a lawyer and judge. As a young boy, he served as a page in the household of the archbishop of Canterbury. After pursuing an education in theology and the classics, he studied law at Oxford and was admitted to the bar. His law career eventually led him to elective office in Parliament. Although attracted to monastic life, he decided against becoming a Carthusian monk. In 1505 he married Jane Colt, and they had four children. Jane died at a young age, however, and Thomas subsequently married Alice Middleton, a widow.

A social philosopher, Thomas published his classic book *Utopia* in 1516, an account of an imaginary society ruled by reason. About this time he attracted the attention of King Henry VIII, whom More had tutored as a boy, and the king appointed him to a series of important government positions. He sent Thomas on diplomatic missions to France and Flanders, and in 1517 appointed him to the royal council. In 1529 the king named him Lord Chancellor, succeeding Cardinal Wolsey. However, Thomas resigned in 1532 in silent protest against Henry's opinions on marriage and the supremacy of the pope. Henry had been greatly irritated when Thomas declined to sign a petition to the pope requesting permission for the king to divorce the queen, Catherine of Aragon.

The rest of Thomas' life was spent in writing, including poetry, history, and devotional books. In 1534, with his friend John Fisher (who also became a saint), More refused to swear allegiance to the king as the head of the Church of England. The king put him in the infamous Tower of London prison. Fifteen months later, and nine days after John Fisher's execution, Thomas was tried and convicted of treason.

Thomas told the court that he could not go against his conscience and that he hoped that he and his judges would meet merrily someday in heaven. On the scaffold on July 6, 1535, he told the crowd gathered to watch his beheading that he was dying as the king's good servant, but God's first. Because he sought only the truth in all situations and was willing to speak the truth to those in power, St. Thomas More is an ideal patron for lawyers today.

56

Leaders and Papal Delegates
Blessed John XXIII
October 11

"**G**ood Pope John," as he is often affectionately called, is officially the patron of papal delegates, but he is also a model and mentor for all leaders. Those who find themselves in leadership positions would certainly benefit from learning how this great man shepherded the Church through changing times.

Angelo Giuseppe Roncalli was born on November 25, 1881, the third of thirteen children in a family of peasant farmers near Bergamo. Ordained a priest in 1904, he served as a bishop's secretary and a seminary teacher of church history. Pope Benedict XV named him national director of the Congregation for the Propagation of the Faith. Roncalli then became a papal diplomat, serving in Bulgaria, Turkey, Greece, and France during World War II.

The future pope's leadership skills were evident in the ways he cultivated friendly relations with the Orthodox churches, worked to prevent the deportation of Jews when the Nazis occupied Greece, and dealt in postwar France with the worker-priest movement and bishops who had collaborated with the Nazis. In 1953 he became cardinal patriarch of Venice. He was elected pope on October 28, 1958, just prior to his seventy-seventh birthday.

At the Mass celebrating his papal coronation, John XXIII declared that he wanted, above all, to be a good shepherd. On his first Christmas as pope, he visited prisoners in one of Rome's prisons, where he recalled how one of his own relatives had been incarcerated. He often visited the parishes of Rome as well as hospitals, convalescent homes, schools, and charitable institutions.

On January 25, 1959, Pope John announced that he would convene a Church council, the purpose of which was not to refute errors but to bring the Church into the modern world. The council met for its first session on October 11, 1962. The date later was assigned for the annual liturgical celebration in his memory.

Pope John was noted for his ecumenical outreach. He established the Secretariat for Promoting Christian Unity (now the Pontifical Council for Promoting Christian Unity) and began outreach efforts to the World Council of Churches. Meeting with some Jewish visitors on one occasion, he greeted them by saying, "I am Joseph, your brother."

In September of 1962, Pope John XXIII was diagnosed with stomach cancer. He died on June 3, 1963, before the council had concluded its work. He was beatified by Pope John Paul II on September 3, 2000. His body was moved from its original burial place in the grottoes below St. Peter's Basilica to the Basilica's Altar of St. Jerome, where it is now displayed for veneration.

57

LIBRARIANS
St. Jerome
SEPTEMBER 30

St. Jerome was born Eusebius Hieronymus Sophronius in Stridon in modern-day Croatia about the year 341. He would become the greatest Scripture scholar of his time, but he began his education studying under the famous pagan linguist and scholar of grammar, Donatus. Jerome gained a wide knowledge of the Latin and Greek classics and also became fluent in Hebrew. Although raised as a Christian, he was not baptized until he was eighteen.

In 370 Jerome joined a community of scholars gathered around Bishop Valerian. When a quarrel disbanded the group, Jerome traveled to the East, and in 374 he settled down in Antioch. He had a vision of Christ, and after a serious illness, he lived in the Syrian desert as a hermit for four years. He prayed and fasted while writing. Upon his return to Antioch, he was ordained a priest by St. Paulinus and became active in opposing heretics.

Jerome then moved to Constantinope, where he studied Scripture under St. Gregory Nazianzen. In 382 he went to Rome with St. Paulinus of Antioch to attend a Church council and decided to remain there as secretary to Pope Damasus. In 386 Jerome moved to Bethlehem, where he lived in a cave believed to have been the birthplace of Jesus. There he wrote treatises to refute the writings of various scholars who raised objections to the Christian faith.

Over the course of the rest of his life, Jerome translated most of the Old Testament from the original Hebrew and revised a Latin translation of the New Testament. This is called the Vulgate edition of the Bible, and it was his greatest achievement. In the sixteenth century, the Council of Trent declared the Vulgate the official Latin text of the Bible for Catholics. It was this version that was used for many English Catholic translations until the mid-twentieth century.

From the year 405 until his death, Jerome wrote commentaries on Scripture that were far more advanced than anything written before that time. After a long illness, he died in Bethlehem on September 30, 420. The remains of his body are entombed in the Basilica of St. Mary Major in Rome. He is a doctor of the Church.

Because St. Jerome dedicated his life to books as a means of communicating the word of God and truth in general, he is a suitable patron for librarians. Fittingly, he is also the patron of Scripture scholars.

58

Mental Health Therapists
St. Christina the Astonishing
July 24

*B*orn in a village near Liége, Belgium, in 1150, Christina was orphaned at the age of fifteen. When she was twenty-one, she had an epileptic seizure and seemed to have died. A funeral was held, but during the service, Christina suddenly levitated to the roof of the church. The priest told Christina to come down, and she did. She said that she had visited hell, purgatory, and heaven, and was then allowed to return to earth to pray and suffer for the poor souls in purgatory.

Many amazing events took place during Christina's lifetime. She was said to be able to smell the stench of sin in people, so she fled from them by climbing trees and perching on the thinnest of branches. She would fly up to the rafters of churches or hide in ovens. She would even jump into a fire and cry out in agony, yet remain unharmed.

For most of her life, Christina lived as a homeless woman, dressed in rags and sleeping on rocks. But she served the people of Liége by acting as their conscience. For example, as he lay dying, she told the Count of Looz every sin he had ever committed in his life. If an unjust person gave her something to eat, she would be wracked with pain as she swallowed the food, apparently bearing the suffering for that person's sin.

All these events were recorded by a thirteenth-century Dominican, Thomas de Cantimpré, who had relied on the eyewitness of Cardinal Jacques de Vitry. Some people believed that Christina was insane, while others respected and venerated her. Christina lived the last years of her life in a convent where the prioress said that despite her odd behavior, she was always obedient. She died there on July 24, 1224.

Perhaps Christina's visions of supernatural realities left her mentally unstable. Her life, however, is a reminder that we should view every person with respect and dignity, whatever their affliction. Although there have been great advances in the knowledge and treatment of mental illness, prayers for healing are still part of a Christian's arsenal to fight these diseases, and therapists can turn to this saint as an intercessor for anyone they are treating.

MENTAL ILLNESS
St. Dymphna
MAY 15

According to her legend, St. Dymphna was the daughter of a Celtic chieftain. Her mother died when she was young. When Dympha was fourteen or fifteen, her father, mentally deranged by grief, sought a new wife. He sent his men far and wide in search of a woman that could compare to his late wife, but to no avail. He then turned to his daughter to have as his bride, but Dymphna refused. To combat her father's continuing advances, she escaped with the help of the priest who was her confessor and two companions.

The four traveled to Gheel, Belgium, where they adopted the life of hermits. Dymphna's father tracked her down and at once killed the priest and her other two friends. When Dymphna refused to return with him, he beheaded her. She died about the year 640.

In the thirteenth century, the relics of the four martyrs were rediscovered. Soon word circulated that prayer for Dymphna's intercession often resulted in the healing of the mentally ill and those with epilepsy, and many began making pilgrimages to her shrine.

In a miracle unto itself, the village of Gheel became dedicated to the healing and assistance of the mentally ill. In some places it is often difficult to get even a residential care facility located in a neighborhood. In Gheel a hospital for the mentally ill has been in existence since the thirteenth century. Because this hospital became overcrowded soon after it was established, the people of the village opened their hearts and their homes to those suffering from mentally illness. The afflicted were accepted as members of the family and were also given work to do as a way of helping them move toward healing. This custom continues in Gheel today. The residents of Gheel, in fact, were centuries ahead of their time in caring for the mentally ill by deinstitutionalizing them.

Many believe that the existence of this community and the healings that take place there can only be attributed to the intercession of St. Dymphna and the grace of God. After all these centuries, Gheel continues to set an example of devotion to the healing of people with mental illnesses.

60

THE MILITARY
St. Joan of Arc
MAY 30

St. Joan of Arc was a peasant girl born in eastern France around 1412. When she was thirteen years old, she began to hear voices—which eventually became visions of Sts. Michael, Catherine, and Margaret—that told her that God was calling her to save France. The voices became more insistent until finally, when she was sixteen, she met with the eldest son of the deceased King Charles who had yet to claim his throne. Joan told him that God had sent her to help him defeat the English. He believed her and fitted her with armor. She famously led the French army into battle at Orleans, where they defeated the English in 1429. A few months later, Charles was crowned.

However, in 1430 Joan was captured by French opposition forces, who sold her to the English. Joan was put on trial by a Church court, which condemned her as a heretic. On May 30, 1431, when she was nineteen years old, she was burned at the stake.

The French armies eventually pushed the English out of France. Twenty years later, King Charles ordered a new trial, and Joan was declared innocent. In 1920 Joan was canonized by the Church that had once excommunicated her. She was already considered a saint in the eyes of the French people, and she remains a signifi-cant figure in French and Western culture.

Joan's military service was motivated by her faith and was an expression of it. Her boldness, courage, and single-mindedness can inspire all Christians who serve in the military today—especially women who serve in so many different capacities in the armed forces. Joan is also the patron of the U.S. Women's Army Corps and U.S. WAVES (Women Appointed for Voluntary Emergency Service).

61

MISCARRIAGES
St. Catherine of Sweden
MARCH 24

St. Catherine of Sweden was the fourth of the eight children of St. Bridget of Sweden. Born at Ulfasa, Sweden, around the year 1331, Catherine was thirteen when she was married to Eggard von Kürnen. They jointly agreed to a vow of celibacy. In 1350 she traveled to Rome to visit her mother, who convinced Catherine that she should remain with her. After Catherine's husband died later that year, she refused proposals of marriage from numerous men.

For the next twenty-five years, she lived with her mother. The two used Rome as a base to make pilgrimages, including one to Jerusalem. When they weren't traveling, they spent their days in prayer and in caring for the poor and sick. When Bridget died, Catherine went to Vadstena, a convent in Sweden that Bridget had founded. There she served as abbess, devoting herself to organizing the Bridgettine nuns. The following year she went to Rome and eventually received the approval for this religious community from Pope Urban VI. She also sought the canonization of her mother.

Catherine's health was failing as she returned from Rome to Vadstena, and she died there on March 24, 1381. In 1484 Pope Innocent VIII approved the veneration of Catherine as a saint. Although Catherine was a virgin, Pope Innocent declared her the patron of women at risk for miscarriage and of women who have experienced the sadness of a miscarriage.

62

Missionaries
Thérèse of Lisieux
October 1

Thérèse Martin, often called the "Little Flower," is a beloved saint whose spirituality, called her "little way," has had a profound impact on the Church in modern times.

Thérèse was born in the town of Alençon, France, on January 2, 1873. She was the youngest of the nine children of Louis Martin and Zélie Guérin, of whom only five survived beyond infancy. Louis was a watchmaker, and Zélie died in 1877 when Thérèse was four years old. The family moved to Lisieux, and Thérèse was raised by her older sisters. When two of Thérèse's sisters entered the local Carmelite convent, she declared that she would do the same. She applied for acceptance at the Lisieux Carmel when she was fourteen but was refused because she was too young. A year later, however, she was accepted and took the name Thérèse of the Child Jesus.

Thérèse lived the ordinary life of a Carmelite nun. Although she had a strong desire to become a saint, she felt she was incapable of doing great things on her own. So she decided to trust completely in God's mercy and surrender to him so that he could do the work of making her a saint. For her part, she offered sacrifices to God in small ways. For example, she made it a point to greet the most cantankerous sisters with a sweet smile.

Thérèse threw herself into prayer for foreign missionaries and adopted two spiritual "brothers"—priests to whom she wrote and encouraged in their missions. For this reason, she is patron of missionaries—even though she spent her entire adult life in the Carmel in Lisieux.

In 1895 Thérèse experienced the first symptoms of tuberculosis. Following a long period of both spiritual and physical suffering, she died on September 30, 1897, at the age of twenty-four. Her spiritual autobiography, *The Story of a Soul*—written at the request of her superiors in her last years—was first published in 1899 and quickly became an international best seller.

Before she died, Thérèse promised to "spend my heaven doing good on earth" and "let fall a shower of roses." After her death, stories circulated of the appearance of roses and their fragrance, along with miraculous healings and answered prayers.

When Thérèse died, the official policy of the Church was to wait at least fifty years before a cause for canonization for sainthood could begin. This policy was waived in Thérèse's case, and she was beatified in 1923 and canonized two years later—less than twenty-eight years after her death. In canonizing Thérèse, Pope Pius XI declared that she became holy precisely in the midst of, and by means of, the ordinary events of everyday life. In 1997 Pope John Paul II declared her a doctor of the Church.

63

Mothers
St. Monica
August 27

Monica lived in North Africa in the mid-fourth century, from approximately 331 to 387. Although a Christian, she married a pagan named Patricius who was known for having a violent temper. The couple had three children—Augustine, Navigius, and Perpetua. Through her patient prayer and example, in 370 Monica's husband and mother converted. Patricius died the following year.

Most of what we know about Monica comes from Augustine's timeless classic, the *Confessions*. At the age of seventeen, Augustine moved to Carthage to study and lived a dissolute life for years. He embraced Manichaeism, a dualistic blend of various religions and philosophies that taught the existence of two eternal principles, good and evil. Augustine also lived for years with a woman to whom he was not married and fathered a child with her.

During all the years that Monica prayed persistently for her son, she was comforted by a dream that Augustine would come to know the truth. When Monica once told a priest of her troubles with Augustine, he told her that it would be impossible for the "son of so many tears" to be lost.

Monica followed Augustine to Milan, where both were influenced by the bishop, Ambrose. Finally, in 386 Augustine converted and was baptized on Easter the following year. Augustine attributed his conversion to the persistent prayers of his mother. Monica lived with her son and a group of his friends at Cassiciacum while he prepared for baptism. The two were in Ostia, Italy, awaiting a ship to take them back to Africa when both mother and son had a mystical experience of God's love. Monica died in Ostia but felt that her life's purpose had been fulfilled.

Monica was buried at Ostia, but her relics were taken later to Arrouaise, where the Augustinian Canons promoted devotion to her. In 1430 some of the relics were moved to Rome, where they are kept in a church dedicated to St. Augustine. St. Monica is an inspiration to all mothers—indeed, all parents—who have children who are far from God. There are numerous groups of mothers that gather to pray for St. Monica's intercession for their children. Here is one prayer to St. Monica:

Exemplary mother of the great Augustine, you perseveringly pursued your wayward son, not with wild threats, but with prayerful cries to heaven. Intercede for all mothers in our day so that they may learn to draw their children to God. Teach them how to remain close to their children, even the prodigal sons and daughters who have sadly gone astray. Amen.

64

MOTORISTS
St. Frances of Rome
MARCH 9

The daughter of a wealthy couple of noble lineage, Frances of Rome was born in the Trastevere section of Rome in 1384. She was married at the age of thirteen to Lorenzo Ponziani—against her wishes as she wanted to enter the convent—but her forty-year marriage was successful. At the time it was not fashionable for noble women to serve the poor. However, Frances found a kindred spirit in her sister-in-law, Vannozza, and together they devoted many hours each week to prayer and to caring for the poor of Rome.

When a plague and famine afflicted Rome, Frances did all she could to alleviate the suffering of the people. She even sold her jewelry to provide assistance to victims of the plague. However, the family's finances suffered when an antipapal army of Ladislaus occupied Rome in 1408 and Lorenzo was wounded in the fighting. In 1410, when Ladislaus again occupied the city, Lorenzo was forced to escape, although the women were able to remain. The Ponziani castle was looted by Ladislaus' soldiers, and the family properties in the Campagna region were burned. Two of their six children died of the plague.

Peace was finally restored to Rome in 1414, and the family's properties were returned. Lorenzo was able to return from banishment, but his health was permanently damaged. Frances nursed her husband and continued to work at her charitable activities. She also organized the Oblates of Mary. Loosely affiliated with the Benedictines of Monte Oliveto, the women in the community lived a secular life with no religious vows but were dedicated to serving the poor.

Lorenzo died in 1436, and Frances entered a convent that she had established several years earlier for the Oblate women who wanted to live in a community. She experienced many visions and ecstasies, brought about many miraculous cures by her prayers, and had the gift of prophecy. During the last twenty-three years of her life, she was guided by an angel only she could see. She died on March 9, 1440, and was canonized in 1608.

On her feast day, priests bless cars and drivers. Of course, St. Frances never drove a car, but she is the patron of motorists because of the angel that preceded her when she traveled at night. The angel's lantern kept her safe on her journey.

65

MOUNTAIN CLIMBERS
St. Bernard of Montjoux
MAY 28

*B*orn about the year 923, Bernard became a priest and was appointed vicar general of Aosta in the Italian Alps. For more than forty years, he was a missionary in this region, bringing the gospel to the people in the Alps who lived in remote areas and had no access to the sacraments.

St. Bernard is most remembered, however, for his care of pilgrims traveling through the dangerous passes of the Alps. He established an Augustinian monastery at the highest point of a pass across the Pennine Alps, which went from the valley of Aosta to the Swiss canton of Valais. The pass was covered with snow all year round and in the spring was subject to avalanches. In 962 he built a monastery and hospice at the highest point—8,000 feet above sea level. The pass eventually became known as the Great St. Bernard. He established another monastery and hospice at what became known as Little St. Bernard Pass through the Graian Alps at 7,000 feet above sea level.

All year round but especially during heavy winter snowstorms, the Augustinian monks, accompanied by their well-trained dogs, went in search of travelers who might have succumbed to the cold and snow. The monks offered food, clothing, and shelter to those they rescued, and they buried the dead, relying on gifts and collections for their support.

The final good deed of St. Bernard's life was the reconciliation of two noblemen. He died in 1008 in Novara, Italy. Although venerated from the twelfth century in northern Italy, Bernard wasn't canonized until 1681. He was proclaimed the patron saint of mountain climbers by Pope Pius XI in 1923. His image appears on the flag of some detachments of the Tyrolean Alpine Guard. The dogs used by the monks are descendents of the modern-day St. Bernard breed.

MUSICIANS
St. Gregory the Great
SEPTEMBER 3

*T*he son of a rich Roman nobleman, Gregory was born around 540 and was educated in Rome. He had been appointed to the office of prefect of Rome when the Lombard invasion of Italy threatened Rome in 571. Since youth he had sensed a call to the religious life. In 574 he remodeled his home into a monastery named for St. Andrew and became a monk. He also established six other monasteries on his estates in Sicily.

In 578 Pope Pelagius II ordained Gregory a priest and appointed him to be one of the seven papal deacons. Between 579 and 585, he served as papal nuncio to the Byzantine court but was called back to Rome in 586. He returned to the life of the monastery and was elected abbot of St. Andrew's soon thereafter. A plague struck Rome in 589–590, and Pope Pelagius was one of those who died.

Gregory was elected as the new pope. He soon began a program of reform, putting Church disciplines in place, removing inept, ineffective, or corrupt priests from official offices, and forbidding priests from taking fees for funerals and ordinations. He also established a widespread program of charitable works for the poor. He protected Jews from persecution and fed the victims of famine. Gregory was responsible for the conversion of England to Christianity, primarily because he sent St. Augustine of Canterbury and forty monks there as missionaries from his own monastery of St. Andrew's.

While placing a great deal of emphasis on the principle of papal supremacy in the Church, at the same time Gregory preferred for himself the title "Servant of the Servants of God"—a title used by popes to the present day. Gregory was an eloquent preacher; he also wrote treatises, hundreds of sermons, and letters. In addition, he also actively encouraged the development of Benedictine monasticism.

Gregory is patron of musicians because he had such a profound influence not only on the Church's liturgy but also on liturgical music. He established a school for chanters in Rome known as the *schola cantorum*. Several hymns are also attributed to him. Because he restored the ancient chant of the Church, Gregorian chant as sung today is so named in his honor.

An early recipient of the title doctor of the Church, Gregory is also considered the founder of the medieval papacy. He died in Rome on March 12, 604, and was canonized by popular acclamation immediately after his death.

67

NURSES

St. Catherine of Siena

APRIL 29

The daughter of a dyer and the second youngest of twenty-five children, Catherine was born on March 25, 1347, in Siena, Italy. She became a lay Dominican when she was sixteen. Until she was twenty-one, she lived a secluded life in her home, where she spent hours in prayer and had many mystical experiences.

Then God called her to a more active ministry. She spent much of her time caring for the sick in hospitals, especially those with serious diseases such as leprosy and cancer. During a terrible outbreak of the plague in Siena in 1374, Catherine and her associates worked night and day to care for those stricken.

Her compassion for the dying was not limited to those who were sick, however. Catherine made a habit of visiting condemned people in prison, hoping they would turn to God. Once she walked to the scaffold with a young man from Perugia who was sentenced to death for speaking publicly against the government of Siena. His last words were "Jesus and Catherine!"

Celebrated for her gifts as a peacemaker, she traveled to Avignon, France, where in 1376 she convinced Pope Gregory XI to return to Rome. She spoke out against corruption in the Church and deeply mourned the papal schism that occurred before her death.

While visiting Pisa in 1375 she received the stigmata—the wounds of Christ in her hands, feet, and side. These remained invisible, however, until the time of her death.

On April 21, 1376, Catherine suffered a stroke and died in Rome on April 29. A book she dictated while in ecstasy, called *The Dialogue*, is a conversation between God and a "soul" and reveals the depth of God's love and mercy for his people. Some four hundred of Catherine's letters are still in existence. Catherine was canonized in 1461, and she was declared a doctor of the Church in 1970 by Pope Paul VI.

PARENTS
St. Louis IX of France
AUGUST 25

B orn in Poissy, France, in 1214, King Louis IX was a model Christian monarch for his era. The future saint became king when his father, King Louis VIII, died in 1226. Louis was only twelve years old, so his mother, Queen Blanche, served as queen-regent until Louis was twenty-one. When he was fourteen, he married Margaret of Provence, who was thirteen. Together they had eleven children.

Louis IX ruled France during a time of many positive social and cultural developments, including the construction of magnificent Gothic cathedrals and the establishment of great universities. Louis was exceptionally generous to the poor. He often distributed food to them himself, and he founded a hospital to care for the poor and destitute. In the carrying out of justice, he was often very merciful. Between 1245 and 1248, he built the famous Sainte-Chapelle in Paris as a shrine to house the relic of Jesus' crown of thorns. He also founded three monasteries.

From our perspective, Louis IX also had some serious faults. For example, he declared that Jews were deliberately and knowingly rejecting the true faith and encouraged the public burning of the Talmud.

In 1248 Louis sailed with his army to Cyprus to conduct a crusade in the Holy Land. The crusade turned out badly, and he was captured. Louis paid a ransom so that he and other prisoners could be released, and after visiting a few of the holy places, he returned to France in 1254. He organized another crusade in 1270, but when he arrived in Tunis, he contracted typhoid fever and died there on August 25 of that year. His bones were shipped back to France and buried at the subsequently famous abbey church of Saint-Denis in Paris.

Miracles reportedly took place along the route of Louis' remains on the journey back to France and again at his tomb. He was canonized in 1297. In 1298 his bones were removed from the tomb and sent to various important personages and churches. During the French Revolution, the bones that remained in the original tomb were pillaged, scattered, and lost. Eventually other remains were located and placed in a reliquary in the cathedral in Carthage, near where he had died.

Because he was the father of eleven children, Louis IX is the patron of parents as well as parents of large families. Parenting is a heroic vocation—and even more so when families are large— so saints who were parents are especially sensitive to our prayers for intercession.

69

Penitent Sinners
St. Mary Magdalene
July 22

Mary was a disciple of Jesus from the town of Magdala, on the western shore of the Sea of Galilee near Tiberias. Traditionally she has been the classic example of the repentant sinner, a role derived from her identification with the unnamed woman who anointed Jesus' feet in the house of Simon (Luke 7:36-50). She has also been identified with Mary, the sister of Martha. There is no evidence in the gospels to support these identifications, however. Modern Scripture scholars do not believe they are the same woman.

Jesus cast out seven demons from Mary Magdalene (Mark 16:9; Luke 8:2), and she was one of the women who "provided" for Jesus and the disciples "out of their resources" (Luke 8:3). She was also one of the women present at the crucifixion (Matthew 27:56; Mark 16:1-8; Luke 24:1-10). In three of the gospels, she is the first person to see the risen Christ (Matthew 28:9; Mark 16:9; John 20:1-8).

According to legend, Mary Magdalene was buried at Saint-Maximin in what is now Provence, France. Her relics are kept in a magnificent bronze casket in the crypt of the basilica there, which dates from the late thirteenth century.

Mary Magdalene was a devoted follower of Jesus. She stood at the foot of the cross during Jesus' crucifixion, and after his death, she hurried to the tomb with spices to anoint his body. She was rewarded with being the first to see the risen Jesus. Whether or not she lived a sinful life before meeting Jesus, her life changed dramatically after her encounter with the Lord. Surely she is a powerful intercessor for all of us who need the grace of daily repentance and conversion.

PHARMACISTS
Sts. Cosmas and Damian
SEPTEMBER 26

Cosmas and Damian were twin brothers, born in Arabia in the middle of the third century, and physicians who practiced medicine but never took any fees from their patients. In the Orthodox Church, they are known as the *anargyroi*, which is Greek for "moneyless ones." Countless cures were credited to the brothers. One famous story says they were able to graft the leg of a recently deceased man onto a patient whose leg had become ulcerated.

Since they did not hide their Christian faith, around 287 they were arrested during the persecution of the Roman emperor Diocletian. Brought before the governor of Cilicia, they were tortured and beheaded in Cyrrhus, Syria. A basilica was built in their honor, and veneration of the two spread through the Christian world.

A second church was built in honor of Cosmas and Damian in Constantinople during the fifth century, and a third in Rome in the sixth century. Pope Felix IV arranged for their relics to be brought to Rome and constructed a basilica by connecting two pagan temples. It was probably about this time that the names of Sts. Cosmas and Damian were included in what is now called the First Eucharistic Prayer of the Mass. Later six more churches in Rome were dedicated to Cosmas and Damian. As devotion to them spread, many other churches in Greece—and in Eastern Europe in particular—were dedicated to them.

Not surprisingly, Cosmas and Damian are also patrons of surgeons and physicians. Their generosity in treating people for free has been a tradition in the Church for centuries and continues to this day. Many in the medical profession today donate time to treat people in free clinics, both in the U.S. and overseas. We can ask these two saints to intercede for those with healing gifts to continue to be generous to people in need.

Physicians
St. Pantaleon
July 27

Pantaleon was martyred for his Christian faith in the early fourth century. According to tradition, he was the son of a pagan father and a Christian mother who raised him in the faith. He became a physician and eventually was appointed the official physician of the Roman emperor Maximian. As time passed he grew to enjoy the corrupt life of the emperor's court.

Then a Christian named Hermolaos brought Pantaleon back to his faith, and Pantaleon began to give freely of his medical skills to the poor. He was known for curing many people miraculously. When the next emperor, Diocletian, launched a persecution of Christians in 303, fellow physicians denounced Pantaleon. He was arrested with Hermolaos and two other Christians. All three were condemned to death, but Pantaleon even cured someone during the trial. Pantaleon was miraculously saved from death by six methods of execution, including drowning, wild beasts, and fire. Finally he was beheaded.

The Orthodox Church calls Pantaleon the Great Martyr and Wonder-Worker. He came to be regarded as the patron of physicians in the Middle Ages. The stories of his miraculous cures remind us that God can heal us, both through the skilled hands of the physician and the prayers of faith-filled Christians.

POLICE OFFICERS
St. Michael the Archangel
SEPTEMBER 29

St. Michael is one of the three archangels, with Gabriel and Raphael, who are venerated in the liturgy of the Church. Michael, whose name means "who is like God," makes two appearances in the Old Testament as a helper to the Israelites (Daniel 10:21 and 12:1). He is named twice in the New Testament (Jude, verse 9; Revelation 12:7-9).

Michael puts in many appearances in Hebrew apocryphal literature. Church tradition early on identified Michael as the angel in charge of all the other angels and the protector of Christians against Satan—in particular at the hour of death, when he guides the soul to God. One tradition declares that Michael gives a final chance to each dying person to repent and be saved, which causes great perplexity to the devil. Michael is also described as the heavenly helper of Christian armies against their enemies.

Veneration of St. Michael the Archangel began in Phrygia in what is modern-day Turkey, but devotion to Michael soon caught on in the West. It grew further from the story that Michael appeared on Mount Garganus in northern Italy during the papacy of Gelasius (492–496) and pointed out a location where a shrine was to be built in his honor. Churches have been dedicated to St. Michael as early as the fourth century.

One legend says that Michael appeared dramatically at the mausoleum in Rome of the emperor Hadrian in response to prayers during an outbreak of the plague, at which time the plague ended. Since then the mausoleum has been named the Castel Sant'Angelo in honor of Michael. Michael reportedly appeared to the emperor Constantine. St. Joan of Arc declared that Michael was one of the heavenly guides who emboldened her to save France from the English during the Hundred Years War (1337–1453). And St. Thomas Aquinas included Michael in his discussion of angels in his monumental *Summa Theologica*.

Typically St. Michael the Archangel is portrayed holding a sword and fighting with or standing victoriously over a slain dragon. His feast day is known as Michaelmas Day. The most famous shrine to Michael is Mont Sant-Michel in Normandy, France, where a Benedictine abbey was established in the tenth century. Many groups have adopted St. Michael as their patron, but he is particularly well-suited for police officers, whose job it is to protect the public.

73

PRIESTS
St. John Vianney
AUGUST 4

St. John Vianney spent his life as a parish priest ministering to the people of the small town of Ars, France. It was a backwater village, and when he arrived, he found few believers among the 230 inhabitants. So effective was his example of holiness and his ministry, however, that not only did the townspeople have a change of heart but penitents from all over France also flocked to his confessional. Today the Church honors this saint as a model for the priesthood.

Jean Marie Baptiste Vianney, also known as the Curé of Ars, was born in 1786. He grew up working on his father's farm at Dardilly, near Lyons, France, and attending secret—and illegal—Masses. Because the French Revolution had interrupted the educational system, John had no formal education and struggled with his studies. He had particular difficulty learning Latin. Fortunately, he found a private tutor in a parish priest, and in 1815 he was ordained.

For two years he served as an assistant to his old tutor. Then in 1817 John was sent as parish priest to Ars, where he remained for the rest of his life. His preaching, his example of prayer and penance, and especially his gift as a confessor had a great effect on the town: Most of the villagers turned back to their faith. It was said that in the confessional, he could read consciences. He cared for the poor, refurbished the church, and started an orphanage that he called the Providence. In the years just prior to his death, he spent as many as sixteen hours a day in the confessional. At its height, some twenty thousand visitors came to Ars each year.

John Vianney died on August 4, 1859, at the age of seventy-three. He was canonized in 1925. In 1959 Pope John XXIII wrote an encyclical on St. John Vianney to commemorate the one-hundredth anniversary of his death. In 2009 Pope Benedict XVI declared a Year for Priests and made St. John Vianney the universal patron of priests, calling him "a true example of a pastor at the service of Christ's flock."

74

PRISONERS
St. Dismas
MARCH 25

Dismas is the name traditionally given to the "good thief" crucified with Jesus on Calvary. The other thief is known as Gestas, but neither name occurs in the New Testament. *The Arabic Gospel of the Infancy of the Savior*, which was popular in the West during the Middle Ages but is not based in fact, included a story about the two thieves holding up the Holy Family on their way to Egypt. According to this story, Dismas buys off Gestas with forty drachmas to leave them unmolested. Then the infant Jesus predicts that they will be crucified with him in Jerusalem and that Dismas will go with him to paradise.

Dismas is the patron, not only of prisoners and those on death row, but also of various ministries carried out on behalf of those in prison. These groups serve the spiritual needs of prisoners by providing prayer, hope, and comfort. Many conduct retreats within prisons to bring inmates into a personal relationship with Jesus and to provide a sacramental presence through confession and the Eucharist. St. Dismas, who turned to the Lord at the very end of his life, gives hope to all those who have spent a lifetime away from God: Our Father offers us the gift of mercy at every moment of our lives, no matter what we have done before. It is never too late to turn to him.

75

Pro-Life Movement
Blessed Margaret of Castello
April 13

*B*lessed Margaret of Castello was born in 1287 to a noble family in the castle of Metola, southeast of Florence. She had multiple birth defects: She was blind, hunchbacked, and a dwarf with a malformed short right leg. Ashamed of her, Margaret's parents locked her in a cell adjacent to a forest church. Although she could not go out, she was able to attend Mass and receive the sacraments. When she was fourteen, her parents took her to the tomb of a holy man named Fra Giacomo in the village of Città di Castello, where miracles were reportedly happening, to pray for a cure for her handicaps. When no miracle happened, they abandoned Margaret in a church.

Margaret was adopted by a group of women who found her. Later she was taken to a convent. However, her sincere faith and dedication to an austere lifestyle caused the nuns, who were used to a rather comfortable life, to send her away. Taken in by a villager, she became a lay Dominican. She cared for the poor, the sick, and prisoners, many of whom responded to her kindness by returning to the Church. Reports circulated that miracles sometimes followed Margaret's prayers.

When Margaret died in 1330, the great crowd at her funeral demanded that she be buried inside the church, but the priest refused. However, a girl disabled by an accident was miraculously cured during the funeral, and the priest relented.

Margaret did not allow her disabilities to lead her to self-pity or bitterness. Instead, she focused on the love of God and brought that love to those around her. An unborn baby found to have birth defects today often is aborted before birth. Margaret's life is a demonstration of why we should honor all people, even those with physical and mental challenges. Margaret is a patron not only of the pro-life movement but of those with disabilities.

In 1558 Margaret's remains were moved because her coffin had decomposed. Her clothes were also decomposing, but Margaret's body was incorrupt. She was beatified on October 19, 1609, by Pope Paul V.

76

Public Relations
St. Bernardine of Siena
May 20

St. Bernardine was a Franciscan priest in the fourteenth century and one of the greatest preachers of his time. He traveled ceaselessly across Italy, working for peace between warring cities and attacking rampant paganism. He attracted huge crowds, sometimes as many as thirty thousand people.

Born on September 8, 1380, Bernardine grew up in Siena, Italy. When he was twenty years old, he volunteered to take charge of a hospital during a plague. With the help of other young men whom he recruited, he cared for the critically ill for several months. Then he gave another year to nursing a beloved aunt. When she died, he began to fast and pray with the intention of discovering God's will for his life.

When he was twenty-two, Bernardine joined the Franciscans and two years later was ordained a priest. For about twelve years, he lived in prayerful solitude. However, when his gift for preaching became known, his superiors sent him out to be an itinerant preacher. Always traveling by foot, he sometimes preached for hours in one location. Then he would move on to preach in another town. Even though he had a weak voice that was often hoarse from overuse, he accomplished great things for Christ. Miraculously, often after his voice was virtually gone from speaking, it would return—which he attributed to his devotion to the Blessed Virgin Mary.

Bernardine became known in particular for his devotion to the Holy Name of Jesus, and he designed a symbol, IHS, which stood for the first three letters of the name of Jesus in Greek. This he placed in Gothic letters with a blazing sun as a background. Bernardine came up with this symbol specifically as an alternative to the popular superstitious and divisive political symbols of his time. This devotion to the Holy Name of Jesus spread, and Bernardine's design soon appeared in many places, both sacred and secular.

Some churchmen opposed Bernardine's symbol because they thought it a dangerous theological novelty. Three times well-meaning priests and theologians tried to get the pope to reprimand Bernardine, but the Franciscan's holiness and adherence to orthodox beliefs were clear evidence of his authentic Christian faith.

Bernardine became superior general of one branch of a Franciscan order, the Friars of the Strict Observance. He placed an emphasis on the value and importance of scholarship and the study of theology and canon law. When he first took office, there were three hundred friars in the community. When he died on May 20, 1444, membership totaled four thousand. During the last two years of his life, Bernardine returned to his first love, preaching, and he died in Aquila while on one of his missionary journeys.

Bernardine's IHS symbol is an early instance of the modern ways advertisers and public relations professionals have learned to best communicate information. He is patron for both groups.

77

RACIAL JUSTICE
St. Martin de Porres
NOVEMBER 3

Martin de Porres was born out of wedlock in Lima, Peru, on November 9, 1579. His father was John de Porres, a Spanish knight, and his mother was Anna Velasquez, a Panamanian freed slave. When he was baptized, he was registered as the son of an unknown father and was therefore considered illegitimate. At that time, illegitimacy was a distinct social and economic disadvantage.

At the age of twelve, he became a barber's apprentice. In 1594, when he was fifteen, he became a lay helper for a Dominican community in Lima. In 1603 the superiors of the community eliminated the rule that excluded black people from receiving the Dominican habit or taking vows, and the future saint became a Dominican brother.

Martin fulfilled various duties, including serving as barber, infirmarian, and wardrobe keeper. He was also dedicated to serving the sick, and he established an orphanage and a hospital for children. He was given charge of his community's distribution of food to the poor of all races, and he ministered to African slaves brought to Peru for sale. He also established a shelter for stray cats and dogs and nursed them back to health. Martin wanted to become a foreign missionary and suffer martyrdom, but his efforts in this regard were frustrated. Instead, he dedicated himself to a life of prayer and penance: fasting, eating no meat, and spending much of the night in prayer. He was a close friend of St. Rose of Lima.

The people loved him for his efforts to help the poor and for his deep spirituality and holiness. According to some accounts, he had the gift of bilocation (of being in two places at once) and could fly through the air. He had a reputation for spiritual insight and for the gift of healing. His fellow Dominican friars held him in high esteem, but he often referred to himself in derogatory terms.

After suffering from a high fever, Martin died on November 3, 1639, just days before his fortieth birthday. Immediately after his death, Martin became the object of widespread veneration. He was canonized in 1962 by Pope John XXIII, who noted that Martin helped many black people and those of mixed race "who were looked upon at that time as akin to slaves." Martin "deserved to be called by the name the people gave him: 'Martin of Charity,'" the pope added.

The work of achieving racial justice is ongoing, and it often starts with a change in people's hearts. As patron of race relations and racial justice, this saint is a gift to the Church, upon whom we can rely in the struggle to erase prejudice in our time.

78

RAPE VICTIMS
St. Maria Goretti
JULY 6

Maria Goretti was born on October 6, 1890, the daughter of a poor family of farm laborers who worked for a landowner near Nettuno in central Italy. Maria's father, Luigi, her mother, Assunta, and the five other children lived in the same building as another family, Giovanni Serenelli and his teenage son, Alesandro. In 1900 Luigi died of malaria.

On July 5, 1902, twenty-year-old Alessandro found Maria— then nearly twelve—in a room by herself, sewing. He threatened to kill her if she did not allow him to rape her. Maria refused, however, declaring that what he wanted to do was a mortal sin and that he would go to hell. She resisted Serenelli with all her strength and screamed over and over, "No! It is a sin! God does not want it!"

Serenelli first choked Maria, but when she declared that she would rather die than submit to him, he stabbed her eleven times. The wounded girl tried to get to the door of the room, but Serenelli stabbed her three more times and ran away.

The commotion and noise woke up Maria's little sister, Teresa, who started crying. When Serenelli's father and Maria's mother arrived, they found the bleeding Maria and took her to the nearest hospital in Nettuno. Doctors operated on Maria, but her injuries were too serious for her to survive. As she lay dying, Maria forgave her attacker and said she wanted him to be with her in heaven. She died twenty hours after the attack, while looking at a picture of the Blessed Virgin Mary.

Alesandro Serenelli was soon arrested and imprisoned for the murder. While in prison, he had a dream of Maria handing him a bouquet of lilies, which burned in his hands. This experience, as well as a visit from the local bishop, produced a change of heart. He was released early from prison for good behavior, and in 1936 he visited Assunta and asked for her forgiveness. He eventually joined the Franciscan Third Order.

Forty miracles were attributed to Maria's intercession after her death, and the cause for Maria's sainthood was opened. In 1950, when Pope Pius XII canonized Maria Goretti, Alessandro was present for the canonization ceremony.

In our own era, rape has often been used as a weapon against innocent women caught between warring factions in various parts of the world. Also an issue in our own time is human trafficking, in which girls even younger than Maria Goretti are sold as prostitutes. It is certainly appropriate to pray today for the intercession of St. Maria Goretti on behalf of all victims of rape.

RETREATS
St. Ignatius of Loyola
JULY 31

Now and then everyone needs time apart from ordinary life to focus in prayerful ways on his or her relationship with God. The general term for such times is "retreat," because the idea is to step away from our regular concerns, quiet our spirits, and open ourselves to the inspiration of the Holy Spirit.

The gospels tell us that Jesus himself made time to go off and be alone with God. Many saints set such an example as well. Perhaps the saint who has most influenced what happens in a retreat is St. Ignatius of Loyola, the founder of the Society of Jesus.

Born in 1491 to a noble family in the Basque region of Spain, Ignatius was the youngest of thirteen children. When he was sixteen, he became a page to the treasurer of the kingdom of Castile and was quite fond of the courtly life. In 1521, while he was a military officer, he was seriously injured by a French canonball that struck his right leg. He was so vain that when his leg healed with one bone protruding below the knee, he requested that it be broken again and reset.

While recuperating, he read and reflected on the gospels and the lives of the saints and was deeply moved. Determined to dedicate his life to Christ, he recovered and went on a pilgrimage to Montserrat. Then he made an extended retreat from 1522 until

1523 at Manresa. It was here that he wrote most of his great classic, the *Spiritual Exercises.*

Following several years of university study, at the age of forty-three, Ignatius and six companions (including St. Francis Xavier) took vows and then traveled to Rome to dedicate themselves to the service of the pope. The new order was approved by Pope Paul III in 1540, with Ignatius as superior general. The Jesuits became missionaries and teachers and founded hundreds of schools and universities all over the world. Ignatius died in Rome in 1556 and was canonized in 1622. The *Spiritual Exercises* are still used by religious and laypeople alike as a guide for discernment and for growing closer to Jesus.

Many of us have difficulty finding time to carve out of our busy lives for a retreat. If this is your situation, pray for the intercession of St. Ignatius to motivate you so that you can attend a retreat and spend some quiet time with God.

80

Sailors
St. Brendan the Voyager
May 16

*B*rendan is one of the most popular Irish saints. He was born about the year 484 near Tralee, Kerry. As an infant he was cared for by St. Ita. When he was six years old, he was sent to a monastery school, and in 512 he was ordained a priest.

Brendan established many monasteries in Ireland. The most famous of these was Clonfert, which he founded about 559 and which became a center of missionary activities for centuries afterward. About three thousand monks lived there under Brendan's direction as abbot. He himself undertook missionary journeys, not only in Ireland, but in England and Scotland as well.

He became famous for his voyages—in particular a seven-year voyage to the "Isle of the Blessed," an earthly paradise recounted in the epic saga titled *The Voyage of St. Brendan the Abbot.* This work was very popular during the Middle Ages and was translated into most of the languages of Europe. Historians and other scholars for a long time seriously doubted that such a mid-sixth-century voyage actually took place. Today, however, some have suggested it could have happened as the story claims and that the Isle might actually have been North America.

Brendan probably died about the year 577 while on a visit to his sister, Brig, who was abbess of a community of nuns. He is also the patron saint of sailors and travelers. At the United

States Naval Academy in Annapolis, Maryland, there is a large stained glass window that commemorates his achievements. At Fenit Harbor in Traleee, Ireland, a large bronze sculpture has been erected in memory of Brendan.

It is well established historically that Columbus was looking for St. Brendan's Isle when he discovered the West Indies. As a student at the University of Pavia, Columbus would have learned of Brendan's voyage from the manuscripts brought there seven hundred years earlier by the founder of the university. The day before his voyage in 1492, Columbus wrote: "I am convinced that the terrestrial paradise is in the Island of St. Brendan, which none can reach save by the will of God."

SCHOOLCHILDREN
St. John Bosco
JANUARY 31

St. John Bosco was a beloved priest, educator, and writer whose ideas about teaching and caring for children were revolutionary for his times. John was born in 1815 in a small town near Turin, Italy. His father died when he was two years old, and his childhood was spent in near destitution. As a young boy, he had a dream that his life's work would be to care for unruly children, "not with blows, but with charity and gentleness." When he was sixteen, he entered the seminary and was ordained a priest in Turin in 1841.

The young priest soon began his lifelong dedication to caring for and educating lower-class boys, mostly in Turin, which was becoming industrialized. After being chased out of one neighborhood because of the noise level of the boys who flocked to him, he and his mother found a place to house and educate them. He opened trade schools to train boys in becoming shoemakers, tailors, printers, bookbinders, and ironworkers. John was very successful, and by 1856 he was housing and caring for 150 boys with another 500 cared for by ten other priests. John believed in using love and encouragement rather than restraint and punishment to teach and motivate his students. He also gave the boys religious instruction. He collected funds to support his ministry by preaching, authoring popular books, and begging for donations to support his work.

Other priests joined John in his ministry to poor and homeless boys, which led to the beginnings of a religious community. Encouraged by a professor at the Turin seminary, in 1859 John founded the Society of St. Francis de Sales, popularly called the Salesians, so that his work would continue after his death. This community was approved unofficially by Pope Pius IX in the same year and received official approval in 1884. With St. Mary Mazzarello, he organized a similar community for women called the Daughters of Our Lady Help of Christians, or the Salesian Sisters. At the time of his death on January 31, 1888, there were nearly one thousand Salesian priests and nine hundred sisters.

More than forty thousand people stood in line to move slowly past his body as it lay in a simple casket in a church. Reports at the time declared that the entire city of Turin filled the streets for the beloved priest's funeral. St. John Bosco was canonized by Pope Pius XI on Easter Sunday in 1934. The next day, Italy held a national holiday in honor of St. John Bosco.

We can turn to John, not only for the example of his life and his intercession, but also for his writings on how to educate and raise children. His philosophy of treating difficult children with kindness rather than toughness has certainly been validated by modern-day educators and parents—which is perhaps why he is still relied upon today.

SCIENTISTS
St. Albert the Great
NOVEMBER 15

Possessing one of the great minds of the medieval Church, Albert was among the first and greatest of natural scientists. He had an extensive knowledge of biology, chemistry, physics, astronomy, and geography—indeed, one of his treatises proved that the earth is round. He also wrote voluminously on logic, metaphysics, mathematics, Scripture, and theology. He was the first to apply the writings of Aristotle to the teachings of the Church—a project taken up from him in brilliant fashion by his student, Thomas Aquinas.

The eldest son of the count of Bollstädt, Albert was born about the year 1206 in the family castle in Swabia, Germany. Even as a boy he impressed his teachers with his intelligence. In 1223 he was sent to study at the University of Padua in Italy, where he entered the Order of Preachers (the Dominicans), even though his family objected. By 1228 he was teaching at the University of Cologne. He then taught in four different cities in Germany, and when he returned to Cologne, he already had a reputation for being a great scholar.

Albert moved to the University of Paris, and one of his students in both Paris and Cologne was the young Thomas Aquinas, who was also making a reputation for himself as a great scholar. The two Dominicans were to become lifelong friends, and Albert later defended Aquinas against attacks from other theologians.

In 1254 Albert was elected provincial of the Dominican Order. Two years later, he traveled to Rome to repel the attacks of those who were criticizing orders with traveling preachers and teachers, including both the Dominicans and the Franciscans. While in Rome, Albert became personal theologian to Pope Alexander IV. He resigned as provincial in 1257 so that he could dedicate himself to scholarly work. In 1260, despite his objections, he was named bishop of Regensburg; however, he resigned two years later so that he could return to teaching.

In 1274 Albert was called upon to participate in the Council of Lyons, a failed effort to bring about the reunion of the Orthodox Church with Rome. On his way there, he received word that Aquinas had died, and he declared that the light of the Church had gone out. In 1278, in the midst of his continuing defense on behalf of Aquinas and his scholarship, Albert suffered from memory lapses. He died in Cologne on November 15, 1280.

St. Albert the Great was canonized and simultaneously declared a doctor of the Church by Pope Pius XI in 1931. Because of his cutting-edge work in science for the times, he is the patron of scientists. His natural curiosity, penetrating insight, and desire to learn about the natural world on the one hand, and his life of holiness and dedication to God on the other, are a living testament to the Church's belief that there is no inherent conflict between faith and reason. Scientists today can look to their patron for guidance in navigating this controversial area.

83

Searchers of Lost Articles
St. Anthony of Padua
June 13

St. Anthony of Padua was a great Franciscan preacher from the Middle Ages, but he is most remembered as the finder of lost or stolen objects. Even today stories are told by people who recover lost articles following prayer for the intercession of St. Anthony.

The reason for invoking St. Anthony's help stems from an incident in the saint's life. Anthony had a book of psalms that he cherished. Any book before the invention of the printing press was of great value, but this one also included the notes he used when he taught students in the Franciscan Order. A novice who had grown weary of the religious life decided to leave the community, and on the way out he took Anthony's book of psalms. When the future saint noticed that his book was missing, he prayed that it would be found and returned to him. After this prayer the novice returned the book to Anthony and also returned to the order.

Anthony was born Ferdinand de Bulhoes in 1195 in Lisbon, Portugal. He was the son of a knight who served in the court of King Alfonso II of Portugal. As a boy he studied under the priests of the Lisbon cathedral. When he was fifteen, he entered an Augustinian monastery, where he was educated. He was ordained an Augustinian priest in 1219. A year or so later, he met some Franciscan missionaries on their way to Morocco to preach to the Muslims. The friars were later martyred, which so inspired Anthony that he asked permission to transfer to the Franciscan Order. It was granted, so he took the name Anthony and set off for Morocco to be a missionary. He returned the following spring because of health problems. His ship, which had been headed to Portugal, was caught in a storm so he ended up in Italy.

Anthony was assigned to work in a kitchen in St. Paul's Monastery near Forli. One evening he was called to give an extemporaneous sermon. His preaching was so powerful that he was sent to preach all over Italy. His sermons attracted huge crowds, and soon he spent all his time preaching. In 1226 he moved to Padua. He reformed the city by attacking corruption wherever he saw it. He did all he could for the poor, struggled to abolish debtors' prisons, and engaged in dialogue with those opposed to orthodox Christianity, frequently winning them over.

In 1231 Anthony became seriously ill and died on June 13. He was just thirty-six years old. Anthony was canonized the following year, and in 1946 he was declared a doctor of the Church by Pope Pius XII.

SECOND MARRIAGES
St. Adelaide
DECEMBER 16

A delaide was an empress of the Holy Roman Empire in the early Middle Ages. Her life at court was a story of intrigue and betrayal, but she did much to support the work and growth of the Church.

Born in 931, Adelaide was the daughter of King Rudolf II of Upper Burgundy (today western Switzerland). When she was sixteen, she married King Lothair of Italy, but only because the marriage was among the terms of a treaty between her father and Lothair's father. Lothair died in 950 from poisoning, and suspicion fell on the man who succeeded him, King Berengarius.

Adelaide was imprisoned when she refused to marry King Berengarius's son, but she was later freed by the German king, Otto the Great, when he invaded. Adelaide married Otto in Pavis, a town in southwestern Lombardy in northern Italy.

Otto became emperor of the Holy Roman Empire in 952, and Adelaide was crowned empress. Otto died in 973 and was succeeded by his son, Otto II. Twice she was banished from the court by her daughter-in-law, the Byzantine princess Theophano. When Theophano died in 991, Adelaide returned and served as regent for her grandson.

Adelaide dedicated herself to the founding and restoration of monasteries and to working for the conversion of the Slavic peoples to Christianity. She died on December 16, 999 in a monastery she had founded in Selz near Cologne, Germany.

Because of her marriage to Otto, Adelaide became the patron saint of second marriages. In our time second marriages often follow divorce and a Church annulment. Of course, second marriages also happen following the death of a spouse. In either situation, it always makes sense to pray to St. Adelaide for her intercession for the success of a second marriage.

85

SEPARATION FROM A SPOUSE
St. Nicholas von Flüe
MARCH 21

The Flüeli is a fertile plain near Sachseln in Switzerland, so this saint's name indicates his place of origin. Born in 1417, Nicholas married Dorothea Wissling and had ten children. He served in the army, fought in a war, and held offices in the civil government, although he refused when offered the office of governor.

In 1467, at the age of fifty and with the consent of his wife and children, Nicholas became a hermit. He is said to have lived the last nineteen years of his life taking no nourishment except the Eucharist each day. His reputation for holiness and wisdom was widespread, and a steady stream of both ordinary people and prominent citizens sought him out for advice and spiritual guidance. In 1481 he helped to avoid a civil war. On March 21, 1487, he died in his cell. He was canonized in 1947 by Pope Pius XII.

Nicholas' patronage of those who are separated from a spouse goes back to his own frequent absences from home and family. It may certainly be some comfort to have this saint to turn to during those times when spouses must be apart. He is also the patron saint of Switzerland. He is known there as "Brother Klaus" and is considered to be the most outstanding religious figure in Swiss history.

In a discussion on the implications of faith and our use of created things, the following words of this saint are quoted in the *Catechism of the Catholic Church* (226):

My Lord and my God, take from me everything that distances me from you.
My Lord and my God, give me everything that brings me closer to you.
My Lord and my God, detach me from myself to give my all to you.

86
Single Mothers
St. Margaret of Cortona
February 22

The daughter of a farmer, Margaret was born in the town of Lavinio in the Tuscany region of Italy in 1247. Her mother died when she was seven years old, and Margaret was raised by an unkind stepmother. When she was seventeen, she ran away from home and became the mistress of a young nobleman, later giving birth to a son. Nine years into this relationship, the nobleman was murdered, and Margaret decided to reform her life. She returned to her home but was not well received, so she and her son went to Cortona. She declared her sins publicly in the church in the town of Cortona, where she had gone to seek the aid of Franciscan friars.

Margaret and her son were taken into the home of two women, Marinana and Raneria. After a three-year probationary period, she was accepted as a lay Franciscan, and two Franciscan priests became her spiritual advisers. The priests supported Margaret during these three years and tempered the strict penances that she was inclined to adopt.

When she first arrived in Cortona, Margaret earned a living nursing sick women. But after she became a Franciscan, she began caring for the poor and sick of Cortona free of charge. Spending much of her time in prayer and contemplation, she experienced deep spiritual joy and visions of Christ, who called her "*poverella*," or "poor little one." She became a peacemaker and on several occasions took to task corrupt Church officials. In 1286 Margaret received the approval of the local bishop to establish a religious community of women who called themselves the *Poverelle* to care for the poor and the sick. She built a hospital in Cortona and founded a lay association, the Confraternity of Our Lady of Mercy, to support the hospital. Her son became a Franciscan friar.

In her later years, Margaret spent most of her time in contemplation. When she died in 1297, she was immediately declared a saint by popular acclamation even though her formal canonization did not take place until 1728. Her incorrupt body lies in St. Basil Church in Cortona.

Being a single mother is no easy task, either in Margaret's day or in current times. Single moms and dads need our support. In Margaret's life, the support of the women and friars in Cortona led her to a life of prayer, service, and holiness. May we also be on the alert to support single mothers whom we encounter in our own lives.

87

Social Workers
St. Louise de Marillac
March 15

Wife, mother, and founder of a religious community, Louise de Marillac was a remarkable woman who partnered with St. Vincent de Paul to extend the network of care for the poor and sick throughout France and eventually throughout the world.

Louise was born out of wedlock in Paris on August 12, 1591, and never knew her mother. Her father was a member of the aristocracy, and she was given a good education by Dominican nuns in Poissy. Although she wanted to join a religious community, she was refused entrance. In 1613 she married Antoine le Gras, an official in the royal court, and they had one son, Michel. When Antoine fell ill, Louise struggled with depression. In 1623 she had a vision of herself serving the poor and living in a religious community. In her vision she also saw a priest, who would later turn out to be St. Vincent de Paul.

Antoine died in 1625, and that same year Louise met Vincent de Paul, the priest in her vision. After several years of giving her spiritual direction, he invited her to assist him with the Confraternities of Charity in the parishes of France. Her organizational and management skills, as well as her deep spirituality and desire to serve Jesus, made her an effective co-worker of St. Vincent's. In 1633 she began to train young women to help the poor and invited them to live with her in her home. The fledgling religious community became known as the Daughters of Charity, and grew rapidly to serve those in need in hospitals, orphanages, and homes for the elderly. The order was approved by the pope in 1655.

When Louise died in Paris on March 15, 1660, her sisters were in more than forty houses throughout France. Today the congregation has more than 25,000 members all over the world. Louise was canonized in 1934, and in 1960 Pope John XXIII named her the patron of Christian social workers. For social workers today, Louise is a model of how to combine a life of active service with a life of prayer—and why both are necessary to truly serve those in need.

SONGWRITERS
St. Caedmon
FEBRUARY 11

*L*iving in what is now England in the mid-seventh century, Caedmon was a lay brother who worked as a herdsman at Whitby Monastery in North Yorkshire. According to an account of his life by St. Bede, one night the brothers were singing hymns. Since Caedmon did not know any, he went back to tending the animals. That night in a dream, he received the verses of a hymn in praise of God, which he remembered the next morning. He also wrote down additional verses.

Shortly thereafter Caedmon took monastic vows and was taught Scripture and doctrine by the scholars at the monastery. According to Bede, whatever Caedmon learned, he turned into a beautiful hymn.

Considered the first Anglo-Saxon writer of religious poetry, St. Caedmon is also known as the father of English sacred poetry. Only one of his hymns survives, the one that he was given in the dream:

Now [we] must honor
the guardian of heaven,
the might of the architect,
and his purpose,
the work of the father of glory

—as he, the eternal lord,
established
the beginning of wonders.
He, the holy creator,
first created heaven as a roof
for the children of men.
Then the guardian of mankind
the eternal lord,
the lord almighty
afterward appointed
the middle earth,
the lands, for men

89

Stress

St. Padre Pio of Pietrelcina

September 23

Padre Pio is a well-known modern saint who lived the spirituality of the cross. "Pray, hope, and don't worry" was one of St. Padre Pio's favorite sayings, which makes him the ideal saint to turn to during stressful times. He certainly was subject to many stressful situations in his own life.

Francis Forgione was born on May 25, 1887. His parents were poor farmers who lived in the village of Pietrelcina in southern Italy. He was a devout child, and in 1903 Francis entered the novitiate of the Capuchin Franciscans. When he received the habit of the Capuchins, he was given the religious name of Pio (in English, Pius). Following seven years of academic studies, the young friar was ordained a priest in 1910 at the age of twenty-three.

In 1912 Padre Pio experienced, on an intermittent basis but invisibly, the wounds of Christ or stigmata in his hands, feet, and side. Although they could not be seen, they were painful and swollen. In 1916, after spending several years with his family because of poor health, Padre Pio was sent to the friary in San Giovanni Rotondo, where he lived until his death in 1968.

On September 20, 1918, when Padre Pio was thirty-one years old, the stigmata became visible and remained so until not long before his death. Not surprisingly, Padre Pio was the object of intense investigation by medical professionals. Many attempts were made to heal the wounds, but nothing had any effect. The wounds remained completely free from both healing and infection for fifty years.

During his long life, Padre Pio was noted for his many extraordinary deeds, including miraculous healings, the ability to know the sins of penitents before they confessed them, and bilocation. For several years, while investigating the reports of these supernatural phenomena, the Church prohibited him from saying Mass or hearing confessions. He considered the greatest achievement of his life to be the establishment and construction of a hospital in San Giovanni Rotondo in 1956.

Padre Pio died on September 23, 1968. One hundred thousand people viewed his body and participated in the funeral liturgy. The beatification of Padre Pio took place in May of 1999, and Pope John Paul II canonized him on June 16, 2002, in the presence of half a million people

90

TEACHERS
St. John Baptist de la Salle
APRIL 7

St. John Baptist de la Salle was a brilliant innovator and reformer of education who founded a community of consecrated laymen devoted to teaching. Born on April 30, 1651, in Rheims, France, he was the oldest of ten children of a wealthy family. He began his studies for the priesthood at the age of eleven and studied at Saint-Sulpice Seminary in Paris from 1670 to 1672. He was ordained a priest in 1678 and sent to Rheims, where he met Adrian Nyel, a Catholic teacher who was about to open a school for poor boys. In 1683 John gave his inherited fortune to the poor and dedicated himself to teaching poor children and training teachers.

When John formed a lay religious community called the Institute of the Brothers of the Christian Schools, twelve of his student teachers followed him. He set up a junior novitiate in 1685 for younger men who wanted to join the community, which came to be known as the Christian Brothers.

John revolutionized education in many ways. He set up "normal" schools all over France specifically designed to train teachers. He established a network of schools across the country that grouped students by ability and taught them in their own language rather than in Latin. He also founded a reformatory for boys at Dijon in 1705, and in 1717 he established a school for adults in prison.

John resigned his position as head of the Christian Brothers in 1717, and on April 7, 1719, he died at St. Yon, Rouen, where he had retired. He was canonized in 1900 by Pope Leo XIII, and in 1950 Pope Pius XII named him the patron saint of teachers. His dedication, his desire to meet the needs of all his students, and his willingness to "think outside the box" are an inspiration to teachers today who are striving to fulfill such a worthy calling.

91

Teenagers
St. Aloysius Gonzaga
June 21

*A*loysius Gonzaga was a Jesuit seminarian who died at the young age of twenty-three. Although he desired to be a missionary, he never traveled to foreign lands to preach the good news. He was ill for much of his life. However, his holiness and purity made such an impression on those who knew him that he was beatified only fourteen yeas after his death.

Born on March 9, 1568, Aloysius was the first son of a nobleman who was in the service of King Philip II of Spain. His father wanted Aloysius to have a career in the military, but even as a boy he expressed a desire to enter religious life. In 1577 he was sent to Florence to be educated, and there he joined the court of a nobleman. Subsequently he contracted a kidney infection that resulted in digestive problems for the rest of his life. He began to spend considerable time in prayer, and he gave religious instruction to the poor.

While serving in the court of the prince of the Asturias in Spain, Aloysius expressed a desire to join the Society of Jesus and become a missionary, but his father refused. Aloysius and his father returned to Italy in 1584, and he continued to seek his father's permission to enter the order. Eventually his father agreed. Aloysius renounced his right to succession of the family property and was received into the Jesuit novitiate in Rome at the age of eighteen. He was sent to Milan for his studies but returned to Rome due to his frail health. In 1587 Aloysius took his vows.

When a plague descended on the city in 1591, Aloysius went to a hospital established by the Jesuits to care for the victims. He contracted the plague and recovered, but he was certain that he would die several months later, on the octave of the feast of Corpus Christi. True to his prophecy, he died that day on June 21, 1591.

Aloysius Gonzaga was canonized in 1726 and was declared the patron of young students by Pope Benedict XIII. Pope Pius XI declared him the patron of Catholic youth. Many Catholic schools and universities have been named for him, and he is also the patron saint of AIDS sufferers.

92

TELEVISION
St. Clare of Assisi
AUGUST 11

*B*orn in Assisi on July 11, 1194, Clare was a beautiful woman of noble birth. However, she refused to marry the wealthy nobleman that her parents had chosen for her and was intrigued by the life and teachings of the itinerant preacher of Assisi, Francis.

Deeply touched by a Lenten sermon given by Francis in 1212, Clare ran away from home on Palm Sunday and was received into the religious life by Francis himself. Because Francis did not yet have a convent for women, he found a home for her in a Benedictine convent near Bastia. Her family tried to persuade her to return home, but she refused. Instead, Francis moved her to Sant' Angelo di Panzo convent, and her sister, Agnes, soon joined her.

Clare's father sent twelve heavily armed men to bring Agnes back, but according to the story, Clare's prayers made Agnes so heavy that the men were unable to move her, and she remained there. In 1215 Clare moved into a house that adjoined the Church of St. Damiano in Assisi, and Francis appointed her superior of the community that soon formed. Before long Clare's mother and another sister, Beatrice, joined the community. The women were known as the "Poor Ladies," but after Clare's death, the order was called the Order of St. Clare, commonly known as the Poor Clares.

The community adopted a strict rule of life, including a vow of absolute poverty. In 1228 Pope Gregory IX wanted Clare to accept ownership of some land and buildings. To that end, he offered to free the Poor Clares from their vow, but Clare refused, and her argument was so convincing that the pope gave permission for other convents of the Poor Clares to take the same vow.

The order flourished and spread to other locations in both Italy and France. Clare became so influential that popes, cardinals, and bishops sought her counsel. Many miracles were attributed to her prayers, and in 1241 she received credit for protecting Assisi from an invading army.

Clare died in Assisi on August 11, 1253, and was canonized in 1255. It was said that when Clare was confined to bed in her final illness and unable to attend Mass, an image of the liturgy in the nearby church appeared on the wall of her cell. Because of this miracle, in 1958 Pope Pius XII declared her the patron saint of television. In fact, Mother Angelica, the American nun who launched the Eternal Word Television Network, is a Poor Clare.

THROAT AILMENTS
St. Blaise
FEBRUARY 3

St. Blaise was a physician and the bishop of Sebastea, Armenia. He was martyred around the year 316 by the governor of Cappadocia and Lower Armenia during the persecution of Christians by the Roman emperor Licinius.

According to legend, when the persecution of Christians began, Blaise became a hermit. He was taken prisoner by hunters when it was discovered that he healed sick and wounded wild animals. He was put in prison, then attacked with iron carding combs and beheaded.

The most famous story about St. Blaise is his healing of a boy who was choking because of a fish bone caught in his throat. This was said to have happened as Blaise was going to prison, and afterward, the boy's mother went to the prison to bring two candles to Blaise. From this story comes the ancient and still popular custom of the blessing of throats with candles on the feast day of St. Blaise.

The blessing can come during or after Mass. Two candles are crossed over the throat or head of the person, accompanied by this prayer: "Through the intercession of St. Blaise, bishop and martyr, may God deliver you from every disease of the throat and from every other illness." The annual blessing is seen as a traditional sign of the struggle against illness in the life of the Christian.

94

TOYMAKERS
St. Claude de la Columbiere
FEBRUARY 15

Claude de la Columbiere was a Jesuit preacher and the spiritual director of St. Margaret Mary Alocoque, the French nun who received the revelations of the Sacred Heart of Jesus. At a time when Margaret Mary was in turmoil over these mystical visions, Fr. Claude wisely discerned that the revelations were authentic, and he was instrumental in spreading the devotion all over the world.

Born in France in 1641, Claude joined the Jesuits in 1659, studying in Avignon and Paris. He was ordained a priest and became widely known for his preaching. In 1674 he became the superior of the Jesuit College at Paray-le-Monial, where a Visitation community was also located. When he first preached to the sisters, Margaret Mary heard these words in her heart: "He is the one I sent to you." She then felt free to confide her revelations to him. The heresy of Jansenism, which among other things stressed the depravity of humanity and viewed God as a stern taskmaster, was taking hold at the time. Claude believed that devotion to the Sacred Heart of Jesus would help to combat these beliefs.

In 1676 Claude was sent to England by his superiors to serve as chaplain to Mary Beatrice d'Este, the duchess of York. In the anti-Catholic environment of the time, he encouraged persecuted

Catholics and restored those who had lapsed from their faith. However, he was falsely accused of participating in a plot to assassinate King Charles II, and after being imprisoned for several months, he was banished from the country. He returned to Paray-le-Monial in 1679, but his health failed from the months of imprisonment. He died on February 15, 1682, and was canonized a saint by Pope John Paul II in 1992.

He is the patron saint of toymakers because the main industry in a town in his old diocese named for him is the manufacturer of whistles and toys. Claude is most known, however, for his role in spreading devotion to the Sacred Heart, through which countless people have come to know the great and very personal love of Jesus.

UNBORN CHILDREN
St. Gianna Beretta Molla
APRIL 28

A pediatrician, wife, and mother, Gianna Beretta Molla is a modern-day saint who put her unborn child's life before her own. Because of this loving sacrifice, she is the patron of unborn children and the pro-life movement.

Gianna was born in Magenta, Italy, on October 4, 1922, the tenth of thirteen children. As a student, she was active in the Catholic Action movement as well as the St. Vincent de Paul Society. She graduated from medical school in 1949, and the following year opened a medical clinic in Mesero near her hometown. In December 1954 Gianna met Pietro Molla, an engineer, and they were engaged the following April. They married in September 1955 and had one son and two daughters. Gianna was an active working mom who enjoyed skiing and traveling, saw her medical work as a ministry, and continued to actively serve the Church.

After two miscarriages, in 1961 Gianna was again pregnant. However, during the second month, doctors told her that she had a fibroid tumor on her uterus. In those days doctors treated such tumors with a hysterectomy, which would have ended her baby's life. She chose instead to have the surgeons remove what they could of the tumor without injuring the baby. But several months later, the doctors found that while the baby was healthy,

Gianna had a life-threatening infection, septic peritonitis. On April 21, 1962, Gianna entered the hospital where her fourth child, Gianna Emmanuela, was delivered by Caesarean section. Before the birth, she told her doctors, "If you must decide between me and the child, do not hesitate. Choose the child. I insist on it, save the baby."

A week later, on April 28, Gianna died of the infection. She was thirty-nine years old. In 1994 she was beatified by Pope John Paul II, and in 2004 she was canonized. Her husband and her three surviving children, including the daughter for whom she gave her life, were both present at the canonization ceremony. In his homily, John Paul II called Gianna "a simple, but more than ever, significant messenger of divine love." Another daughter, Laura, said of her mother, "She did not choose death; at that moment she chose the life of her child."

THE UNEMPLOYED
St. Cajetan
AUGUST 7

*B*eing our of work is usually a difficult and stressful experience, particularly if the unemployed person is supporting a
family. It can be a discouraging time and can even tempt one to
despair. St. Cajetan always had a special concern for the poor
and disadvantaged, especially those who were out of work. We
may rely on his intercession in matters both spiritual and practical during those times when we must live with unemployment.

Cajetan was born in 1480 in Vicenza, Italy, to a privileged
family. He studied law at the University of Padua and served in
government positions, first as a senator and later to Pope Julius
II as a protonotary (a type of civil servant in the Church). Both
positions brought him into contact with people who suffered from
social injustice, including the lack of work.

When Julius II died in 1513, Cajetan was admitted to the seminary and was ordained in 1516. He left Rome and returned to
Vicenza. He joined a confraternity called the Oratory of Divine
Love and worked with the poor and the sick, particularly those
with incurable diseases. "In the Oratory, we serve God by worship," he said. "In the hospital, we actually find him." Later he
established similar Oratories in Verona and Venice.

In 1520 he returned to Rome, where he cofounded an institute
of clergy dedicated to reforming the Church, which was known

as the Theatines. He preached widely, cared for the sick, and worked for the reform of a frequently corrupt clergy. This was during the years when the Protestant Reformation was gathering steam, and many of Cajetan's reforms anticipated by decades the reforms that would be brought about by the Council of Trent (1545–1563).

Cajetan also worked with other dedicated priests to found an institute to give extended loans to the poor and unemployed and to combat usury. He died in Naples on August 7, 1547, and was canonized in 1671.

WAITPERSONS
St. Martha
JULY 29

Martha was the sister of Mary and Lazarus. All three were close friends of Jesus, and he probably stayed with them when he was in Jerusalem, which was only two miles away from their village of Bethany.

Martha is well-known for her complaint to Jesus in the Gospel of Luke. Her sister Mary is sitting at the feet of Jesus, listening to his words. Meanwhile Martha is frazzled, trying to get a meal on the table. Martha asks Jesus to tell her sister to help her, but Jesus replies with these famous words: "Martha, Martha, you are worried and distracted by many things; there is need of only one thing. Mary has chosen the better part, which will not be taken away from her" (10:41-42). Thus Martha has traditionally been the model of active Christian service, while Mary is the model of the contemplative. Many a waiter and waitress would do well to call on the intercession of Martha when they are feeling frazzled as well as take to heart Jesus' words to spend a moment with him.

It is Martha who goes out to meet Jesus after the death of Lazarus in the Gospel of John. Even before witnessing Lazarus' resurrection, Martha declares her faith in Jesus (11:27).

A medieval legend says that after the death and resurrection of Jesus, Martha, Mary, and Lazarus went to France and evangelized the region of Provence.

WIDOWS
St. Paula
JANUARY 26

*B*orn on May 5, 347, into a noble Roman family, Paula married a man named Toxotius, with whom she had five children—four daughters and one son. We know about her life through the writings of St. Jerome, who said that she lived in great luxury. Paula and her husband were considered the ideal married couple and lived happily until Toxotius' death in 379.

Paula, who was only thirty-two years old when she was widowed, grieved deeply. Then she met another Roman widow, St. Marcella, and dedicated herself to a life of poverty, simplicity, and helping the poor. She met St. Jerome in 382 when he was in Rome. In 384 her daughter Blaesilla died. A year later she left Rome with her unmarried daughter, Eustochium, for the Holy Land. She settled in Bethlehem with Jerome as her spiritual director.

Paula became Jerome's assistant and confidant and helped him with his biblical studies. She learned Hebrew and, according to Jerome, could chant the psalms in Hebrew without a Latin accent. In Bethlehem she built a hospice for pilgrims and travelers because, unlike Mary and Joseph, she wanted visitors to find shelter. She also built a monastery and a convent where she became abbess. This led to serious financial difficulties for Paula. Today we might say that she overextended herself, but she trusted that God would see her through—and he did. She died in Bethlehem on January 26, 404, and is buried in the Basilica of the Nativity.

Paula serves as an ideal role model for women today who find themselves widowed. When her husband died, she used the time she had at her disposal to serve God, neighbor, and the Church in ways for which she was particularly suited. Her devotion to God also had a great influence on her family: Two of her daughters, Eustochium and Blaesilla, are also venerated as saints.

WINE MERCHANTS
St. Amand
FEBRUARY 6

St. Amand was a French Christian missionary who labored all over Europe, especially in Flanders. He was born in Nantes about the year 584. At the age of twenty, he became a monk at a monastery on the island of Yeu, one of the Ponant Islands and the one most distant from the mainland. Amand was ordained a priest in Tours. For the next fifteen years, he lived as a hermit in Bourges.

When he returned from a pilgrimage to Rome, he was ordained a missionary bishop with no particular diocese. He dedicated himself to missionary activities in Flanders, Carinthia, and Germany. He won many converts after raising a hanged criminal from the dead. Amand was banished because he publicly criticized King Dagobert I. Subsequently the king apologized to Amand and asked him to serve as a tutor for his son. Amand refused.

Instead, he became a missionary among the Slavic people of the Danube. In 649 he was named bishop of Maastricht. When he arrived there, he found rampant heresy and social disorder. With the support of Pope Martin I, he called councils and carried out various reforms. Not long after, Amand resigned as bishop and returned to his missionary activities. Among his many accomplishments was the establishment of a convent at Nivelles in Belgium with the assistance of two women who later became saints themselves: Gertrude and Ita.

At the age of seventy, Amand accepted an invitation to preach in the Basque region and established several monasteries there. He died at the age of ninety at one of the monasteries he had established in northern France, Elnone Abbey in Saint-Amand-les-Eaux.

St. Amand is patron saint of winemakers and brewers because he spent so much time preaching in wine- and beer-making regions.

100

Young Adults and World Youth Day

Blessed Pier Giorgio Frassati

July 4

World Youth Day is a week-long gathering of youth from all over the world that occurs every two years. Started by Pope John Paul II in 1986, World Youth Day attracts hundreds of thousands of young people who gather together to celebrate their faith. The pope always attends, speaking to the throngs of young people and presiding at a Mass for them. Pope John Paul II named Pier Giorgio Frassati the patron of World Youth Day in 1990. When Pope Benedict XVI speaks about World Youth Day, he often holds up Frassati as a model of a young man who was thoroughly engaged in the world yet fully lived out his faith.

Born on April 6, 1901, Pier grew up in Turin, Italy. His family was wealthy and owned the prominent Italian newspaper *La Stampa*. Known among his friends and classmates for his deep religious devotion as well as his fun-loving character and practical jokes, Pier was at home whether attending daily Mass or going on a hiking expedition.

Concerned about the plight of the poor, Pier joined the St. Vincent de Paul Society when he was seventeen. Although his parents were very wealthy and powerful, they gave their children only a modest allowance. Pier habitually gave away his allowance to the poor. He often gave his train fare to beggars and either ran home or rode in the third-class section of the train. He even gave away his overcoat and shoes when he saw someone in need.

However, Pier also believed that his faith required him to be active in social reform. He participated as a leader in student political organizations, and he spoke openly against Mussolini and the Fascist party. He also helped to start a newspaper called *Momento* to promote the social justice principles articulated by Pope Leo XIII in his encyclical *Rerum Novarum*.

In late June 1925, Pier Giorgio Frassati contracted polio. He died on July 4 at the age of twenty-four. His parents and siblings were astonished on the day of his funeral to see the streets of the city packed with thousands of people as the funeral procession passed by. They had no idea of the extent to which he had served the poor. The people of Turin soon called on the archbishop to initiate the cause for Pier's canonization. Turin's young hero of faith was beatified on May 20, 1990.

ALPHABETICAL INDEX OF SAINTS

BIBLIOGRAPHY

McBrien, Richard P. *Lives of the Saints: From Mary and St. Francis of Assisi to John XXIII and Mother Teresa*. San Francisco: HarperOne, 2006.

Bunson, Matthew, Margaret Bunson and Stephen Bunson. *Our Sunday Visitor's Encyclopedia of Saints*. Revised. Fort Wayne, IN: Our Sunday Visitor, 2003.

Butler, Alban, *Butler's Lives of the Saints*. Edited, revised, and supplemented by Herbert J. Thurston, SJ and Donald Attwater. 4 vols. Christian Classics, 1981.

Craughwell, Thomas J. *Saints for Every Occasion: 101 of Heaven's Most Powerful Patrons*. C. D. Stampley Enterprises, 2001.

Delaney, John. *Dictionary of Saints*. New York: Doubleday & Company, 1980. Revised edition 2005.

Saint of the Day: Lives, Lessons and Feasts. Edited by Leonard Foley, OFM. Revised by Pat McCloskey, OFM. Cincinnati, OH: St. Anthony Messenger Press, 2001.

Stevens, Clifford. *The One Year Book of Saints*. Fort Wayne, IN: Our Sunday Visitor, 1989.

HELPFUL WEB SITES

The Patron Saints Index: http://saints.sqpn.com/.

The Catholic Encyclopedia, 1971: http://www.newadvent.org/cathen/.

Catholic Online: Saints & Angels: http://www.catholic.org/saints/.

American Catholic.org Saint of the Day from St. Anthony Messenger Press: www.americancatholic.org/features/saintofday/.

the WORD
among us ®
The *Spirit* of Catholic Living

This book was published by The Word Among Us. For nearly thirty years, The Word Among Us has been answering the call of the Second Vatican Council to help Catholic laypeople encounter Christ in the Scriptures—a call reiterated recently by Pope Benedict XVI and a Synod of Bishops.

The name of our company comes from the prologue to the Gospel of John and reflects the vision and purpose of all of our publications: to be an instrument of the Spirit, whose desire is to manifest Jesus' presence in and to the children of God. In this way, we hope to contribute to the church's ongoing mission of proclaiming the gospel to the world and growing ever more deeply in our love for the Lord.

Our monthly devotional magazine, *The Word Among Us*, features meditations on the daily and Sunday Mass readings, and currently reaches more than one million Catholics in North America each year and another 500,000 Catholics in 100 countries. Our press division has published nearly 180 books and Bible studies over the past ten years.

To learn more about who we are and what we publish, log on to our Web site at **www.wau.org**. There you will find a variety of Catholic resources that will help you grow in your faith.

Embrace His Word, Listen to God . . .

www.wau.org

Santa Clara County
LIBRARY

Renewals:
(800) 471-0991
www.santaclaracountylib.org